T0210061

A PRETEND LIFE, A TRUE STORY

PUSHPA

authorHOUSE®

AuthorHouse™
1663 Liberty Drive
Bloomington, IN 47403
www.authorhouse.com
Phone: 1 (800) 839-8640

Published by AuthorHouse 05/21/2019

ISBN: 978-1-5462-7919-8 (sc)
ISBN: 978-1-5462-7918-1 (e)

Library of Congress Control Number: 2019901337

Print information available on the last page.

ACKNOWLEDGEMENT

I would like to thank all my children and grandchildren for being my rock. It now feels wonderful for me to witness their success and is a great reminder that all the sad, bitter and hard times I went through was all worth it when I see their achievements.

I want to say a special thank you to my daughter, Anjali, who has painstakingly gone through the journey with me to help relay my story.

I also want to thank the lady next door who had helped me whenever I needed her, whose name I unfortunately cannot recall and the nurse in Raleigh where I was working; and for the two strangers who spoke up for me. They have no idea of the appreciation I still have to this day for their help during those rough times and how often I still remember them. They were my angels.

I also want to thank all the potential readers. I hope if you take nothing else away from this story, that you see the importance of perseverance.

PREFACE

I came to Canada in October 1991, at the age of 49 and the same year of my divorce in England. In my mind I was still very hurt, thinking and re-thinking about Sanjeev every day, who was now my ex-husband. His nagging voice which had tormented me while I was with him still rang through my ears. My mind felt trapped by all the negative experiences replaying in my head.

The one tragedy that especially plagued my mind was my rape in India. I was only 13 years old when that happened to me. Not a day has gone by where I haven't felt like cursing him over and over again for taking my innocence away.

I also used to feel pain at the thought of losing my mother when I was 2 years old, and not even having the chance to see or know her, as they had no photos or cameras readily available in India in the 1940's. I, myself, didn't have any photos taken until I was around 27 years of age. However, it made me wish I was adopted, and that I still had a chance to find my mother; like some of the talk show topics, hosted by Montel Williams and later Dr. Phil, where they spoke about children finding their biological parents or parents finding their children who had been adopted.

Even though I am old now, at the age of 76, a mother and a grandmother myself, I often still long for my own mother, so I can tell her all about the painful and insulting life I have lived without her. But I know whatever I wished for, would never happen to me.

One thing I did learn from the talk shows was that talking to someone helps. But sadly, I never had anyone I could trust throughout my whole life. I could not tell my children because it was too shameful for me, therefore I started to write. I wrote whatever I remembered, and although it has somewhat helped me to take things off my mind, I still feel the hurt and disgrace. I wonder if I have done the right thing to release these memories, as they still sometimes linger in the darkness of my thoughts.

But here it is….

CHAPTER 1

I, Pushpa, was born in 1942 in Prangarh Village, a part of the state in Uttar Pradesh (UP), just over 300km from Delhi. I was the youngest of 3 children living with my mother, Rama, grandfather, Lakeraj and aunt, Shanti.

My father, Anand, was away teaching in Punjab, so he only came home every so often. My father was the youngest of one brother and three sisters. My mother had one younger brother and one younger sister and 3 younger half-brothers.

The house belonged to my grandfather which was much larger than our neighbours as we were quite well off. It was a four-bedroom house with a large living room and a huge porch at the front where my grandfather would often sit with his friends. It would have a really nice breeze in the summer and the sun would shine in the early mornings in winter. The bedrooms were all at the back. Only one of the bedrooms had two large windows but the other 3 bedrooms each had an open 8-9 inches circular skylight capped with a slanted top to prevent the rain from coming inside. My grandfather also had a lot of land where he grew many mango trees, along with other fruit trees and wheat farms. My aunt, the oldest of my father's 3 sisters, lived with us because she was widowed soon after getting married. In the early 20th century, widowers could get re-married immediately but widows usually remained with their parents or their brothers' for the rest of their lives.

I was very young when my then pregnant mother became very sick and developed tuberculosis (TB). While sick, she gave birth to my youngest brother, whom she named Ravi, but he soon died at one month old. After my brother's passing, my mother was overpowered by her illness and passed away a month later. She left three children behind: my sister, Veena who was 10 years old, my brother Vijay who was 5, and myself, Pushpa, the very unlucky 2-year-old.

As we were already living with my aunt and grandfather, my father left us again to teach in Punjab. I only have two memories of my aunt, one of them when she was really angry at me, but I don't remember exactly why, except for the fact that I was terrified by her. The second memory I have was very embarrassing to me, so I still remember it vividly. In India people wash themselves with water after going to the toilet. However, for children, the adults help them by pouring water on them as they wash themselves. I remember it was one of those days I asked Veena to pour water on me, but my aunt stopped her from helping me. She told me angrily to go to the pond at the water-well and wash myself there. In India all the water-wells are attached to a 2ft by 4ft pond, so when people fill their buckets with water the extra water spills into the pond so small animals, such as cats and dogs can drink from there. When I went there to wash myself all the women began shouting at me to go home. I was already embarrassed because I was sent there without wearing underwear. But, when I came home my aunt became enraged and shouted at me to go back to the pond. I had no other choice but to go to the water-well and force myself to ignore all the women there and washed myself because the fear from my aunt filled me with more dread. That is the last memory I have of her. I don't remember anything else or even her face.

After two years, my aunt got very sick and died soon after. From what I understand, there was very little medical attention in the village and because of that many people used to die at an early age from fever, malaria and general sickness. I was too young to know exactly how my aunt died.

Now only my grandfather was left to look after us. Since Veena was older, my father thought she could help our grandfather look after us younger children. My grandfather did his best. I was very sick as a child and hated taking medicine. My grandfather used to force medicine down my throat, so I would not die like our other family members. I wish he had not done that because I would have preferred to die. He might have helped me survive, but he himself died with old age two and a half years after my aunt had passed away.

At this time, my father could not come home for my grandfather's funeral because of the curfew imposed all over the country after India received freedom from the British Raj. The curfew was because Gandhiji made Nehru who was a Hindu, prime minister in August 1947, which really upset the Muslims. Fights between the two religious groups broke out. I heard that one of my cousin brother was slashed in the neck but survived with a scar to show the remainder of his life. However, it did not matter whom Gandhiji chose to rule the country - Hindu or Muslim, the fighting was unavoidable as both sides wanted the ultimate power to rule.

A senior colleague and close friend of my father tried very hard to get my father transferred to Delhi which was closer to our village. When his friend finally reached some people in higher positions, my father was finally able to come home.

My mother's father had remarried again but my step-grandmother refused to look after us. My grandfather therefore had to send my mother's aunt, who was already a widow, to look after us. The rest of my mother's and father's families did not care for us. They ran away from us, as far as they could. They called us very unlucky children because so many family members died around us.

When I grew older I understood how right they were to call us "unlucky". Even though my mother's aunt was nice, she could not stay with us much longer as she had to go back home. She asked my father if she could take us with her and he was happy to say yes. It was as if a very heavy weight was lifted off from his shoulders.

The members of my mother's side of the family were farmers. They used to grow everything, including melons. In India, elders are not referred to by their names from children, so we called our mother's aunt "Nani" which means grandmother. She would take Veena to work with her on the farms. Vijay would play on the streets with other children while I had to stay at home with my step grandmother because I was too young to go anywhere.

My step grandmother i.e. step-Nani stayed home because her job was to cook, clean, and do all the housework. I remember when I was hungry, she would cut melons and toss the seeds onto the floor for me to eat. She never gave me any of the melon itself. One time, my Nani came home, and she saw me eating the melon seeds. She asked my step-Nani why I wasn't given proper food to eat and that I must be hungry. My step-Nani answered that I was not hungry, then she looked at me and asked very forcefully, "You are not hungry, ARE YOU?" I knew exactly what she wanted me to say, so I just shook my head and said "no."

I have had very strong childhood memories since I was 2 years old, the things that people said, and the anger in their eyes when they looked at me were terrifying. I could never grasp or understand some of the words that they would say to me, whether good or bad, as I was too young to understand at that time or remember how long we stayed with one family.

As for my grandfather on my mother's side, I don't remember him ever talking to us. Grandfathers from the mother's side were referred to as "Nana". While we were living there Vijay became sick. He hurt his leg and it got infected, so my grandfather did not want to keep us there anymore. He dropped us back to our house in the village where there was no one, except the three of us. When my father heard that we were all alone in the house, he came back to ensure that we would have enough food to stay there comfortably. However, he took Vijay with him, so he could admit him to school while my sister and I stayed alone in the village. I would often get scared to go to the bedrooms at the back of the house as it was dark and scary to me. My father would try to come home to the village to see us and often force me to go to the back to bring or take something there as he thought that would help to take my fear away. He would tell me that I should pray to God any time I would get scared of the dark or of anyone or anything. So, I then started praying any time I was scared, or when someone got angry at me, or made me feel upset or humiliated.

At that time in India, especially in villages, it was not important for girls to have an education. My father also had a very different reason: he said that Delhi was not a safe place for young girls to live. Although there was no longer a fight between the Hindus and the Muslims, there were still bitter feelings between them. We were told that when Muslims see any beautiful, young, Hindu girls, they would kidnap them and take them to Pakistan to marry. We heard it was happening a lot and that it was especially worse in Delhi. For that reason, Veena and I had to stay in our village.

I don't know how long we stayed there, but all I knew was that I have always had an indebted love for my sister for looking after me. I would follow her around because she was the only one I had. Wherever my father sent us, he always sent us together. One time my father sent us for a few days to live with his brother, who also lived in the same village as us. That very first night, his wife set a fire in the kitchen and started screaming and ranting to the neighbors that it was our bad luck that brought fire to her house. She refused to keep us after that, so my father had to take us back to our house where my sister and I stayed alone again.

Later, as my sister grew up, I noticed she no longer wanted me to be around her all the time. She was now a teenager and preferred friends of her own age instead of her little sister hanging around. She got very aggressive towards me if I came near her or did not do what she told me to do. If I forgot to do anything she would hit me. But she was my sister and I still loved her unconditionally even if I didn't think she ever felt the same way about me.

Even though Veena took good care of me, she would still hurt me by keeping me at a distance. Also, whenever I tried talking to anyone, Veena would stop me as she was worried I would get more attention.

My father liked Veena a lot and she was his favorite daughter because they could talk and joke about everything. That is why my father was so happy with her and always talked about her childhood. He did not seem to care about Vijay and my childhood, and it felt as though we had both simply fallen from the sky. I, on the other hand, was scared to talk to him and when I did try, Veena would stop me from the fear of getting our father's attention by elbowing me or pinching me and kicking my leg.

At some point, she made some ragdolls for me to play with to keep me distracted. She wanted to keep me as far away from her as possible so that she could hang out with her friends and leave me home alone. I don't think she realized at that time how young I was and that I had no one to lean on except for her.

Being all by myself, with only ragdolls as playmates, I developed a pretend life in my mind. In this pretend life, I had a mother, a father who had an office job, and two brothers. I named the elder brother Dev, who was 10 years older than me, and I named the second brother Ravi, after my younger brother who had died in real life and who I still longed to have back. I made Ravi 5 years old and myself 2 years old, which was younger than I really was, and called myself Rani. I think at that time I was too young to understand why I created a pretend life but thinking about it now it could have been to fill the gaps of happiness I was missing in my real life. It perhaps fulfilled my longing to have a mother in my life and for a loving father who would be around, as my real father was always away and uncaring. I guess I did not choose a sister because in my real life my sister did not want me around, so I instead created a brother in place of her.

CHAPTER 2

Back in my real life, my father came to take us to live with his younger sister, Garajo for a little while. Her husband was a farmer, and they were not very wealthy. My aunt Garajo was not happy to see us because now she had two more mouths to feed even though my father sent her money regularly to look after us.

I was around 7 years old at the time, the same age as my aunt Garajo's daughter, Daya. Whenever my father visited, he brought two identical dresses, one for me and one for Daya. I always liked to wash my dresses, so they would stay clean, while Daya did not care to clean hers because she had her mother to do things for her. My aunt used to get jealous and look at me meanly while asking accusingly why I was wearing Daya's dress. I would tell her it was mine and that I had washed it. She would give me another killer look even though she knew I was telling the truth.

She would always send me to mix the wheat she put out to dry in the sun. I would have to walk in my bare feet as I didn't have any shoes or slippers to wear in the burning sun to mix the wheat with my hands. Both my hands and feet would get scorched and feel painful. She also made it my job to clean the ash cooker and take the ashes from the baked cow dung to throw out every evening. I would feel hurt that my aunt would constantly make demands on me and never ask Daya to do anything.

She treated Veena better because she was older, communicative and charming. I got treated worse because I was the quiet one and I didn't speak back or defend myself. I didn't even know how to be charming like Veena. I had no voice and no knowledge of how I could speak to people because I grew up suppressed and became very shy and scared. I was always spoken down to and shunned. It made me feel isolated and alone as I felt like I was never loved or protected. That, in turn, made me even more scared of everyone around me and even less confident. Little did I know, this would make me a victim of others reinforcing and abusing their power over me.

My aunt Garajo also had another daughter, in addition to Daya, who was 1-year-old. Although, Daya and I were both barely 7, I was the one who was treated like a nanny, being made to carry the 1-year-old on my hip, all day, and every day. Daya would be playing around happily, while my freedom was taken away by the constraints of caring for the 1-year-old all day as my aunt did her usual chores. I obeyed everyone around me and did everything anyone asked from me without a question. I didn't realize at that time my diligence and loyalty just lead them to mistreat me even more. Instead of any appreciation, my aunt continued with her demands without ever lifting a finger to take care of me, even once. It was still Veena who washed and combed my hair. I would however, take my own baths and wash my own clothes. I remember once, when I was washing my dress near the water-well where they have a large washing area, there was a man who was also washing his clothes. As he did so, the loose pieces of soap would float away, so I picked all the small pieces and used them to clean my dress. He then shouted at me and said, "Why are you using my soap!!" I remember being really scared and unable to say anything to him, but I was totally surprised by a man nearby who defended me and told the angry man off by saying "You already threw those broken pieces, so why can't she use them! She's very smart to use those pieces". I felt very grateful and happy when he spoke out for me but did not have the knowledge at that time to thank him for defending me, which is why I still remember it.

When I was 8 and Veena was 16 years old, my father decided to move us to live with his distant relatives, Girdhar, his parents, his pregnant wife Leela, and their two daughters. They were farmers, and in exchange for looking after us, my father bought them a piece of land for their farming. Girdhar also had four brothers who all lived next to each other, and each of them had 4 or 5 children, whose names I can't remember anymore. Veena was a grown teenager by then and was therefore very happy to spend time with the grownups. I was very happy for the first time as well, because there were children my own age in the neighborhood who were mainly Girdhar's older brothers' children. It felt nice to have real playmates for once. We used to run in the farms and lie on the hay together. In the farms I also loved to eat corn, fresh carrots, and drink sugar cane juice. We used to run around, and play hide and seek as well as look for camel hair in the sand which we considered lucky. There were large plants in the neighbourhood which I used to twist and shape into a horse and carriage, and I became quite creative at making different forms that the other children liked. We used to sleep outside in the summertime and tell each other fairy tales, as well as listen to ghost stories told by the adults. When I think of my happiest childhood memories, those are the only ones that come to mind.

However, because of my bad luck, it did not last very long. Leela and Girdhar already had two girls, so they were overjoyed when Leela gave birth to a boy. But that also meant my childhood was over once again, as I was forced to become a nanny. Leela became persistent and verbally abusive if she didn't see me doing housework or looking after the baby. She would say that I am not doing anything, just wandering everywhere and shaking my breasts around all day. I was only 9 and didn't even have any breasts yet. She would constantly call me very insulting names, and that I am stupid, not capable of doing anything, and so on. I started becoming used to being spoken down to and disrespected.

My cousin Girdhar was mostly nice but whenever I was late bringing his food or if I spilt some water on my way to the farm - which was so far away from the house, he became very angry and called me names. I did not even know what they meant, I just knew that they were not nice words to hear. One day I asked Veena for the meaning of those words. She did not tell me but went straight to Girdhar and asked him why he had said those words to me. He just bent his head downwards in shame and said nothing.

CHAPTER 3

While all of this was going on in my real life, I turned to my pretend life that I created in my mind, where every night before I fell asleep, I would go and start where I had left off the night before. I would return to my parents and two brothers, Dev and Ravi, like I used to. One day in my pretend life, my pretend father's sister came to our house and asked him if she could take my brother Ravi to the fair with her children. My pretend mother never trusted her because she was very greedy, so she said "No," but my father overruled her and let Ravi go with his sister. In the evening my aunt came back without Ravi, crying that she lost him in the fair. She said she looked for him everywhere but could not find him. My parents reported it to the police to find my missing brother, but they did not find him. According to my mother, she thinks my aunt never really lost him but instead she sold him for money. After she lost Ravi, my mother was never the same again. She became very sick and the sicker she got, the further my father stayed away. He started having an affair with his secretary. He was never home and did not care how my mother felt. I was too young to help or do anything for her.

I realize looking at it now, that some aspects of my real life would seep into my pretend life at the early stages of creating it, such as my pretend father not being around for us just as my real father was not.

Back in my real life, my father found a rich businessman's son, named Satish to marry Veena, who was now 18 years old. They lived near Delhi in a town called Hapur. Satish had 2 brothers and 2 sisters. One of his sisters was married and living away. His older brother Ram was working, and both his younger brother and sister were still attending school.

As my father was also very rich he gave a lot of money for Veena's engagement as well as 30,000 rupees for the dowry when they got married six months later. It was a very extravagant wedding and she looked very beautiful. She also received a lot of jewellery from the groom's family and she was very happy and treated well. After Veena got married I became very lonely. Even though she never wanted me to be around her, I still missed her very much. Cousin Girdhar did not want to keep me either, since they already had the land from my father and his son no longer needed taking care of anymore. He suggested to my father that I was missing Veena so that I should stay with her instead. So off I went again.

My father sent Vijay to take me to Veena's house. She wasn't very happy to see me there, but she could not say no to our father. I could not blame Veena for not wanting me there because she, herself, was dependent on her in-laws. Another reason why Veena did not want me there was because her husband was still at university doing his Master's degree while his older brother, Ram, was working in their father's business. This was why Kla, who was married to Ram, would put my sister down by saying that it was only her husband who was working. Kla was Ram's third wife and was very spoiled by her mother-in-law because Ram's first wife died due to sickness and his second wife died during child birth - so whatever Kla said and wanted, she got.

Ram was very nice to me. He always talked to me and gave me attention, which felt nice because I didn't get any before. Veena's mother-in-law was also nice to me. She admitted me to an All-Girl School. Kla became jealous, particularly because I was being sent to school and she could not read or write herself. I was 10 years old in first grade but because I had never gone to school before, it was very difficult for me. When the teachers would explain some of the class material on the board, I would understand everything but by the time I went to write it down on paper, I would forget. The teachers would get very angry at me, especially my Math teacher, who would hit me on the face if I ever made a mistake. She would also pull both my ears and call me names like, "I am a woman growing like a camel." I had been placed in the first grade with the 6-year-old children, so I was obviously taller than them. I was embarrassed myself for being so much older than my classmates which also resulted in them not wanting to be my friend.

Furthermore, I did not get a chance to study or do my homework because as soon as I came home from school, Kla was always waiting for me outside the house. She would hand me her baby daughter, so I would have to take her out. She always kept me busy to stop me from doing school work. She also kept waking me up before daylight to sweep the floor, even though they had house keepers to do that. She would give me her daughter and force me to take her to the neighbours' houses very early in the morning before going to school and as soon as I came back from school. The neighbours started whispering mean things about me and would sarcastically say "here she comes again with the baby!" I was so humiliated but Kla would force me to take the baby every day to the neighbours as there was nowhere else to take her. She didn't care that I was being disgraced and shamed as it made her feel happier.

When bed time arrived, Veena wanted me to do school work, but by then I was so tired and sleepy I could not keep my eyes open. And the next morning, my day would start the same way again.

My own brother-in-law hardly talked to me unless he wanted a glass of water, but his older brother, Ram, would always check my homework, talk to me and make me laugh. I liked him very much and used to wish that he was my own brother-in-law instead, but Kla was very jealous that she would continue to humiliate me every possible way she could. Whenever I ate she would taunt me and say that I had never eaten such good food before I came to live with them. I didn't have the courage to speak back and say that there was in fact nothing special or different about the food. I was used to eating the same, but I just forced myself to say "Yes" to avoid any conflict and keep her happy. When I would dress and comb my hair differently before going to school, Kla would put me down badly and would question me accusingly why I was trying to look "fashionable".

She continuously shamed and hurt me with her cutting voice and her constant demands to the point where I could not bear all the continued insults and condemnation thrown at me daily. She enjoyed inflicting senseless suffering on me and treating me like a servant. She would follow me around and insist I wash everyone's dishes at any time someone used a single dish. I was even scared to have a glass of water. She would scrutinize the house and if she saw anything out of place or dusty, she insisted I clean it immediately. Day after day she made me feel painstakingly miserable that I could not take it anymore. Even if I prayed, like my father had taught me when I was younger, it still did not help me. I felt incredibly hurt and isolated. There was no one to comfort or protect me so I felt powerless to face anyone or anything. I felt as though the only way to release my pain was to kill myself, so I tried to strangle myself until I started choking. Other times I would crush moth balls and drink them. They never killed me, I just threw up.

At the age of 12, and after 2 ½ years of being degraded and humiliated, my father sent Vijay to bring me back from Veena's house to Delhi, where they were living in a rented house. I had never really spent any time with my father or brother when we were children, so we never became close to one another. My father was very neutral and didn't show any love, affection or emotions to both my brother and me. I think by this time I was so numb to any emotions that I don't remember feeling any sense of joy or sadness when I was taken there. He had called me to Delhi as I was old enough to stay home and start cooking and cleaning for them. The house had a long corridor when you entered, one toilet and one storage room on the ground floor and some open space. The second floor had two large bedrooms with balconies, a small kitchen and a full bathroom. He would just tell me what to make for lunch and dinner as he would leave early in the morning to teach at the school. School hours either ran from 7:00-12:00p.m. or from 1:00-5:00p.m. As he used to teach in the mornings he would tutor children after having lunch until late in the evenings when he would come back home for dinner.

Vijay went to college, and I had to stay home to cook for the three of us. Instead of sending me to school, my father used to bring some story books for me to read if I had any time. I used to watch all the neighbors' daughters go to school every morning. I would see them coming back, laughing and talking in the afternoons. I used to wish that I could join them and go to school too. When I asked my father if I could go to school, he made excuses that I was too innocent, or that someone could kidnap me. I asked him instead if I could have a female teacher come home to teach me. His answer was that female teachers were even worse because they made money by selling girls to bad men. But the real reason was greed; he did not want to spend money on me. Also, during that time, some parents thought that girls did not have to go to school, as long as they could read and write. Unfortunately, my father was one of them.

My brother used to nag me all the time, so I did not like him. His nagging also caused arguments between him and our father. My father would send me to the roof top to get some fresh air as I looked really pale, but, my brother would send me back down as he did not want anyone to see me because everyone would usually be out on the roof in the evenings. He was always nagging at me where to sit, where to look. He did not want me to go to the balcony at all to prevent boys from looking at me. He also thought I was very simple and innocent and that someone could easily take advantage of me. My father argued with my brother to let me talk to the neighbors so that I could learn to socialize, but Vijay was old fashioned despite being only three years older. He also blamed me for the deaths of our mother and brother because I was the younger child. I always wished that my brother Ravi survived, and that he would have been a much nicer, loving, and caring brother than Vijay. I may not have any memories of Ravi, but I still missed him very much.

I had so much frustration built up inside of me throughout all my young years, having to live with strangers and obey their rules, accepting whatever they told me. I had to keep all the hurt and pain silenced within me because I had no choice. But, Vijay was my own brother, so for the first time, I could actually argue back. This was something I could never have done with others. But I still loved my brother and always wished him well.

Veena was always happy wherever she lived because she was very social, easy going and good at speaking with everyone, whether they were young or old. In the summer holidays my father would send Vijay to bring Veena to Delhi where we were living. He would spend time with her and enjoyed having her stay with us. He used to talk to her about everything, as well as how he made lots of money. He would explain about investing, buying and selling shares, as well as buying land for farmers. When he used to tell Veena how he made his money, I always listened. They thought I could not understand what they were talking about, but I had a good memory, so later in my life, I used all that information when

I came to England. I started to buy shares and investments, which allowed me to make money and eventually buy my own home.

I would also get very happy when Veena used to come to visit us because I knew I would have someone to talk to, and whether Veena liked it or not, I always wanted to be close with her. I would share my things with her or give the last of anything I had to her, but she would not do the same for me. Even when she would be eating something, if I ever asked to have a little bit, she would totally refuse. An example of this is when Veena would tell me to make her a nice hot paratha with lots of chillies and ghee. I would ask if I could make one for myself, but she would say no because father would ask why we finished all the ghee. So that's when I would ask for a little piece of hers, but she would hit my hand and say that it was all hers. I never expected anything from anyone growing up and was so accustomed to neglect, so I did not feel bad or offended when she said "No" to me.

CHAPTER 4

In my pretend life, my mother was very sick. Some days she would look at me and Dev and start crying while lying in bed. The day before she died, she called my brother and me to her and asked Dev to promise her that he would always take care of me and never let me be sad. Dev was always a very good brother and he kept his promise.

Soon after my mother died, my father started bringing his girlfriend to our home. The girlfriend would eventually bring her own two daughters with her. It was hard watching my father give all his attention to the three of them and hearing that his girlfriend was going to be our new mother. What little bit of attention we got from our father would now be lost forever. I felt upset and jealous, with a sense of loss so deep that it somehow allowed me to gain the power to start seeing through everyone and their false intentions. I saw through my father's girlfriend and her two daughters, and I knew that they were not good-natured and were going to be trouble.

My mother's ashes were hardly cold when my father got married. He said he got married so quickly because he felt we needed a woman to take care of us. When his new wife moved in to our house, she brought her two daughters and her brother called Prem. Prem did not work and could not hold a job because he was an alcoholic. He also liked hanging around gangsters. Our stepmother was very nice to us when our father was home but became like a wicked witch as soon as his back was turned. She would tell me that I was not her daughter and that she did not even like me. Whenever I spilt my drink or dropped any food, she would hit me and take my food away.

In my real life, in Delhi, my mother's brother Raghvir and his family lived one hour away. Whenever I asked my father to go to my uncle's house, he thought it was because I was feeling lonely, so he would take me there and leave me for a few days. But the main reason I wanted to go to my uncle's house was because I wanted to get away from the constant nagging of my brother and the arguments between him and our father. Uncle Raghvir and his wife were both generally nice. Even though they were not very loving, they were always very pleasant as they would talk to me nicely and treat me well.

My uncle Raghvir also had three younger half-brothers: Ramesh, Bhopal and Lala. During one of my visits, uncle Ramesh had come to Delhi to invite uncle Raghvir and his family to celebrate his son's birth. As I was there, he also asked me to come. I wanted to go with uncle Ramesh because he was my favourite uncle whom I liked even better than my real uncle Raghvir. With my father's permission, I joined uncle Raghvir and his family as we all traveled to the village where uncle Ramesh lived. Uncle Ramesh was very joyous and loving and would always show me affection and talk to me. He would tell me about my mother and that I looked like her. He used to tell his wife to make sure I did not wash the dishes and he would actually treat me like a niece. Uncle Ramesh's mother, my step grandmother, the one who used to throw melon seeds for me to eat, would still act very cold towards me when I was there.

After the celebration, uncle Raghvir and his family returned to Delhi, but I wanted to stay longer in the village. I did not want to go back home to my nagging brother. I was later to find out that this would be the biggest mistake of my whole life.

A few months passed, and I had made some good friends and uncle Ramesh was still very nice to me and made sure I was happy - and I really was happy because I could spend time playing with the other girls. It was a village where everyone were farmers and they were also very friendly. We would go to each others' homes and spend time chatting and walking in the warm evenings. I still had regular chores such as going to the water-well with my step grandmother to bring water. She would also tell uncle Ramesh I was bored, even though I was not, just so she could also take me to the fields to carry hay over my head and bring it back to the village to feed the animals. Despite these chores, I was still happier here than back with my father and brother in Delhi - until uncle Bhopal came home from college for his summer vacation.

Uncle Bhopal was 7 or 8 years older than me and was also nice to me until the day of our neighbour's daughter's wedding. I was around 13 years old, watching the wedding with the other girls and he was also watching with his friends, opposite us. I noticed one of his friends, who was very handsome, looking at me. He smiled, and I smiled back. However, it turned out that uncle Bhopal was watching us, and from that day on he started blackmailing me. He claimed that something was going on between me and his friend despite my proclamations. He threatened to tell my father who he knew I was absolutely terrified of. My father was very strict, and I feared that if he believed uncle Bhopal's story he might even kill me. I was always extremely afraid to speak up for myself under normal circumstances and was petrified if my father believed Bhopal's accusation, I would not be heard. Bhopal used my vulnerability and innocence and unashamedly raped me. I felt my heart, life and body shatter and crumble into millions of pieces as he mutilated and victimized the very core of my soul and body. My tears fell into an empty dark abyss as he continued to rape me for two weeks until he went back to college. I could not tell this to anyone. He had ripped out my voice, the little I even had, and just left me feeling ashamed, dirty and disgusted at myself for letting him do this to me.

The rape was too overwhelming for me to face alone. I wanted to kill myself because I did not want the humiliation and dishonour for myself or my family if anyone ever found out I had been raped. One day I jumped from the roof but only fell on the ground damaging my tailbone. I could not walk for a few months and no one took me to a doctor as there wasn't any close by. I also did not get my period for the next 6 months and was filled with the dread and anxiety of being pregnant. I prayed to God that I would get my period and not face the dishonour and the shameful demise at the hands of my father. When I finally got my period, it was the ultimate relief. But I cannot even describe the trauma that this rape caused and has continued to cause me throughout my life.

I was only 13 years of age and was made to feel that my entire existence was a burden. I felt so unwanted, used and abused, manipulated, and now sexually assaulted. I was totally broken. I could not see any reason for my existence. And, it continued to be reinforced in the future by others, that my life was purely futile, and I was better off dead to everyone.

CHAPTER 5

In my pretend life, my step mother did not want us around as she only cared for her own two daughters and her brother. She would buy them new clothes but not for my brother or me. We would end up wearing the same clothes week after week which became old and dirty as she would rarely wash ours. My father either paid no attention to us or intentionally avoided saying anything to his wife to keep her from becoming upset, so she continued to get away with treating us badly.

My happiest moments at that time was when my brother, Dev, came home from school as I felt more protected and less vulnerable when he was around. I could also speak more openly to him and express my feelings. However, when he was not around, my step mother's brother, Prem, would touch me inappropriately and would hit me when I disapproved. His sister, meanwhile, ignored everything. In fact, she hit me more because I would be crying. Sometimes my father would come home while I was crying and would ask me what was wrong, but before I could say anything, my step mother would quickly answer for me. She would say I was crying because I wasn't listening to her. So, instead of comforting me, my father would get very angry and tell me off.

Once, Prem put his hand in my underwear, so I bit his hand until it started bleeding. Prem then started hitting me with a stick and I screamed in pain. That time, my brother came home from school and took the stick from Prem and started hitting him back. There was so much screaming and shouting going on because both Prem and my stepmother started shouting at my brother. Just then, my father came home and without asking any questions, got angry at Dev and ordered him to get out of the house. This was the first time I ever saw Dev getting angry at our father. Dev told him that he never cared about us, and that he was blinded by his new family. And before our father could attack him, Dev lifted me up, stating that he was not going to leave me behind to get tortured by them, and stormed out of the house with me in his arms.

But Dev had no money and did not know where to go. It was getting dark and as we sat in the park, I started to feel ill. We then caught a glimpse of someone walking towards us. When he got closer, we recognized that it was our cousin, Gopal. He was one of the sons of my aunt who had sold my brother, Ravi, but he was very different from the rest of his family. He was friendly and kind and took us to his house. When we arrived, his parents were not so happy to see us. During dinner, he asked his mother if we could eat with them, but she said no and told him to share his own serving if he wanted, and that we could not stay. Gopal sneaked some food for us and gave Dev the two rupees he had in his pocket. Dev refused to take the money, but Gopal insisted, so Dev thanked him for everything he did for us and we left.

Dev did not eat anything that night. He seemed to have something on his mind. He started filling his pockets with stones as he walked with me towards the Jumna River. It had gone really dark when we got there. He then took his shirt off, tied me onto his back with it, and started walking deeper into the Jumna River. Suddenly we heard two voices saying "Son, do not go further. Please come back, we are here to help you." We both turned around surprised to see a couple standing on the river bank, beckoning us to come towards them.

The couple said they had just come from Shiv Temple, where they had been praying for a child for 20 years. The man introduced himself as Vikram and told us he was a police chief. He then introduced his wife, Kamla. They asked if we would like to stay with them, but Dev did not trust anyone anymore, so he looked at me because he knew I could see through people. I nodded yes. Immediately, Kamla took me to a hospital because I was burning with fever. Meanwhile, Vikram took Dev to buy us some clothes as they could see clearly that ours were all dirty and ripped. Afterwards, they brought us to their house which was very big and beautiful. They didn't ask us any questions but instead got us freshened up and gave us hot food to eat and then showed us to our rooms to sleep in.

The next morning, I felt better. Vikram had gone to work and Kamla introduced us to her housekeeper, Ramu. He was a middle-aged man, very soft spoken, and also lived in the house. They treated him like a family member. That evening when Vikram came home we all sat down together for dinner which felt wonderful because we had never sat down for dinner as a family before.

On the second night, before bedtime, they asked Dev what had made him want to commit suicide with me, and why I had so many bruises. Dev hesitated to answer at first, but then eventually told them everything, including what my father's new family had done. Vikram got very angry when he heard this and wanted to put them in jail, especially Prem. But Dev was scared and did not want them to find out where we lived as Prem belonged to a gang and his people could easily locate us. After hearing all that, Vikram and Kamla felt so bad for us. Kamla had tears in her eyes and gave us a big hug and said they would love us to stay with them as long as we wanted.

After some time, when we had settled down and become more comfortable with Vikram and Kamla, they asked if we would be okay with them officially adopting us and changing our names. They suggested changing Dev's name to Danny and my name from Rani to Rajni together with their last name, Bhardwaj. That way, they could send us to school without us fearing Prem and his gang. We of course said yes without hesitation, as it felt like magic to our ears, and we would finally be able to have a real sense of happiness and belonging to parents who genuinely loved and cared for us. They gave us a modern look with stylish haircuts and trendy clothes to wear.

One day, I asked Vikram and Kamla to buy a lottery ticket with the two rupees that Gopal had given us. Much to our surprise, that ticket won us three lakh rupees, so Vikram and Kamla invested the money for us as they did not want to keep it for themselves.

After a while of living my pretend life, I began to think that this life was not so pretend anymore, but rather a happier version of my real life. I realize now that I had inadvertently created a better life in order to escape the sad hardships that I was living in my real life. However, there would be times when some moments would infiltrate in some form or the other as reflection of the hardships I faced in reality. It felt as though I could not even escape the hurt and abuse in my own head. But it turned out that all the triumphs in my pretend life would give me hope and perseverance to carry on living and see a light at the end of the tunnel in my real life.

CHAPTER 6

Back in my real life, in Delhi, my father was searching for a boy for me to marry, so he asked my brother to bring me home from uncle Ramesh's house. My father was considering a 28-year-old doctor for me who he had previously considered for my sister. However, when news travelled to my brother-in-law that my father was looking at marrying me to someone so much older, he wrote an angry letter stating that if my father was incapable of looking after me, then he might as well throw me in the river. My father always respected my brother-in-law, so he started looking for other boys. He did not want me to marry a farmer and end up living in the village, so he searched for an educated boy living in the city. Giving a big dowry was no objection for my father, but all the educated boys were over 20 years old and were also looking for educated girls. My father started blaming me, that I was so unlucky and for this reason he could not find a boy for me. In truth, it was because of him that I was denied the opportunity of having an education. He seemed more interested in saving his money and yet he was ready to give 20,000 rupees away in dowry. In the 1950's, 20,000 rupees was a lot of money. Because of the large dowry my father was offering, many boys' parents would be tempted. However, they would then turn around and say despite how beautiful I was and how much they liked me, they felt I would not understand family values because I grew up without a mother. And, other parents would say they liked everything about me except the fact that I was not educated enough for their sons. They were all educated boys which made me feel worse for not having an education, but the fact that I was very shy also held me back from being able to converse with them openly which may have also affected their decision.

Every time a match failed, my father would get very angry at me. He nagged me all the time for not being able to find a boy, and would often say, "God knows how many crows you ate before you were born to shower such bad luck." It made me feel even worse about myself.

Eventually, my father found a man who had a degree, his name was Sanjeev. He was the eldest of 7 children and lived in Delhi with his father and two brothers, Govind and Mohan. His mother lived in a village around 3 hours away from Delhi with his two younger sisters, Meena and Kamla, and his two younger brothers, Gajinder and Mahesh. His family were poor with old fashioned thinking and lacking manners. And the women in his family were uneducated as they could not read or write their own names.

I got engaged to Sanjeev, and my father spent a lot of money on my engagement. Sanjeev and his parents thought they won the lottery. And, I also thought I would blend in well with his family, even though I was a little bit more educated than the women in his family.

My father later found out that Sanjeev was outspoken, rude and disrespectful, and that his words meant nothing. My father said he wanted to break off the engagement, but Sanjeev and his family became enraged by this. Sanjeev's father started blackmailing my father that they would kidnap me if he did not let me marry his son; they were quite capable of doing anything as Sanjeev's father was extremely mean-spirited and cruel. My father knew once Veena would go back to her own home after my engagement, I would be left alone in the house because he had to go back to teaching and my brother had to go back to school. I was totally oblivious to what was going on at that time, or how demeaning Sanjeev's family was, let alone the blackmailing going on. But, my father still asked Veena to ask me if I wanted to go through with marrying Sanjeev.

Meanwhile, Sanjeev had started writing kind letters to me and sent them with his sister, who began visiting almost every day. He wanted me to write back to him, so I did because he was praising me in his writing, saying that he could not wait to marry me and how beautiful I was. I was fooled by him because no one had ever said good things about me before. So, when Veena asked me if I wanted to marry Sanjeev, I said yes, because I also knew if I did not say yes then my father would continue nagging at me and calling me unlucky. At that time, I also thought that Sanjeev and his family genuinely liked me and was totally unaware that it was all an act while they were blackmailing my father. This was the second worst mistake of my life.

Looking back now, I think my father should never have even considered asking me to choose knowing what he knew. I was only 15-years-old, very naïve and unaware of people's character and behaviour or what they could be capable of. I also could not yet grasp how big of a decision marriage was at that age either.

Once I had agreed, my father told Sanjeev's father that he would only marry me if they agreed my father would not give them any dowry and that I would not live in the village. My father felt strongly about not having any of his children live in the village after my mother died of TB as most of the villages did not have a doctor. People would often have to travel to the city in order to get any treatments. Only a very few villages would have one single doctor but even then, without an appropriate care facility or medicine. Sanjeev's father agreed to all the terms of my father and also promised him that they would move the rest of the family members living in the village to the city in Delhi.

Sanjeev's father rented a big room in a house in Delhi before our marriage to show my father where everyone would supposedly live. When we got married, I was 15 and Sanjeev was 24. My father did not give any dowry, as he had said, but Sanjeev and his father thought that my father was just bluffing, so they felt cheated and insulted. When we arrived at the house after the marriage ceremony, Sanjeev's father started cursing and shouting. He went on all night, calling my father all kinds of bad names. That was my darkest night ever.

Giving dowry was a strong and old custom of the Indian culture throughout generations from rich and poor. It was something that was expected under any circumstances. Looking at it now, I think my father should have known the consequences and disrespect of not giving dowry for my wedding. I think he should have at least given something rather than watching me suffer and pay for his decision at the hands of Sanjeev and his family. I still don't understand how and why my father's ego, or his money, could mean so much more to him then his own daughter's wellbeing and respect. He had many chances to prevent my suffering, but he selfishly chose not to…. I don't think he loved me at all.

Sanjeev's family did not keep their promise to my father either. They had rented the big room and a kitchen for only one week leading up to the wedding and lied to my father about having everyone live there - that was far from the truth. Sanjeev had been living in a very small room on the fourth floor of the house. The room was empty with one small window in it. There were some sheets on the floor to sleep on and that was it. Sanjeev's father and his two brothers had been living on the first floor of the same house. There was only one toilet on the first floor that we all had to use. Sanjeev used to eat with his brothers and father on the first floor so once we were married he bought a small portable coal stove for his room that he placed on one side for me to later cook breakfast, lunch and dinner.

After girls get married in India, the custom is that her brother picks her up on the second day to bring her back home and visit her family to say good bye to all her relatives, who usually wait for her before they head back to their own homes. Her husband then picks her back up after a couple of days. But my brother never even came to take me home. So, on the third day, Sanjeev's mother went back to the village and took me with her while Sanjeev stayed in Delhi. No one asked me if I wanted to go but I could not say no to her. I felt like a cow being led by its owner.

Sanjeev came to the village around a week after to visit, so I asked him to take me to my father's house in Delhi. He said yes, on the condition that I give him all my jewelry and wedding clothes. So, Sanjeev dropped me to my fathers' house dressed unconventionally simple. Usually, the first time the bride visits her parents' house she is overly dressed in lots of beautiful and extravagant jewelry. When Sanjeev brought me back looking so simple, with absolutely no jewelry, my father felt offended. He got very angry at the thought of what people would say if they saw me like that. But he was not only angry with Sanjeev, he was also furious with me for having married him, but I could not say or do anything.

After a few days of Sanjeev not taking me back from my father's house, my father started nagging me again and again, saying that a married girl should not stay at her parent's house for too long. Yet, there I was, unhappily married and sad staying with my father instead of being at my husband's house. I could not say or do anything and was left vulnerable by the customs that dictated the husband has to come and take his bride back from her parent's house. But Sanjeev neither came to get me nor contacted me.

A few months later, Sanjeev's brother, Mohan, came to see me and asked my father if he could take me with him to see my mother-in-law who was visiting her husband and sons living in Delhi because she wanted to speak with me. My father was relieved to say yes. When I went there, my mother-in-law was in Sanjeev's room on the fourth floor, but he was not there. She said he was living at his cousin-sister's house i.e. Sanjeev's uncle's daughter, whom my mother-in-law did not like very much. She said that it was his cousin's and her husband's idea to destroy Sanjeev's relationship with me by encouraging him to say he was going to divorce me to get dowry money. It was considered very disgraceful for a woman to be divorced at that time, so Sanjeev hoped my father would pay up. However, my father refused to be blackmailed and would not give him anything at all, which I was totally unaware of at that time. I now feel pained knowing that my father could have helped my marriage or at least stopped their mistreatment of me instead of watching me struggle, all while blaming me.

Sanjeev's mother also wanted to see me because she felt ashamed that her son was getting divorced soon after getting married. Apparently, rumours had already spread in the village. She wanted Sanjeev to leave his cousin-sister's home and come back to his own. He always refused, so she thought that if she called me, it would be a good reason for him to come back home. So, when she took me to his cousin's house, Sanjeev got very angry and started shouting at his mother the moment he saw me. He told her to take me back to my father's house because he was divorcing me. He argued with his mother and insulted her badly. He was emboldened because his cousin and her husband supported him and had also told him they would find him another girl who was educated and could give him a big dowry. Sanjeev continued shouting at his mother, so she had no choice except to leave with me. I could see how disappointed she was, but I was totally devastated and ashamed thinking how I could possibly show my face to my father. I decided I would throw myself in the river and end all my misery and sadness. My mother-in-law figured it out and asked my brothers-in-law, Govind and Mohan, to watch over me as she did not want to be blamed. Everyone became very nice to me at that time.

After about a month, Sanjeev's brother Govind was getting married. By this time Sanjeev also realized my father was not going to give him anything so he decided to come back home and get involved in his brother's marriage. After Govind's wedding his wife left for the village a couple of days later. As Sanjeev was back, his family started treating me poorly again because I had served my purpose as far as they were concerned. Sanjeev became verbally abusive; he called me all sorts of bad names which I had never heard before. In his eyes, I could not do anything right. Despite everything, I was happier to stay with Sanjeev in Delhi than with my father.

Sanjeev told me that he only married me so that he could have someone to look after his family and then gave me rules to follow. I had to make fresh meals for each member of his family at varying times. He said his brother Govind leaves for work at 5:30 a.m. so I therefore had to get Govind's meal ready by 5:00 a.m. Sanjeev wanted to eat breakfast and take his lunch by 6:30 a.m. and his brother Mohan needed to eat at 7:30 a.m. before leaving for school and his father needed to eat at 11:00 a.m. Back then, there were no gas or electric cookers. I had to cook on a portable coal cooker that would take 45 minutes to 1 hour just to get ready each time. There was no tap, so I had to get water from the third floor to use for cooking as well as bathing, washing clothes, dishes, and cleaning. For this reason, most rooms in India had drainage for that purpose.

Sanjeev did not have any clocks in the house and told me to look at the time in his watch. I was so worried I would not wake up on time, so I would get up every hour to light a match and check his watch. I asked Sanjeev to buy me an alarm clock to help me in the mornings as I would not get enough sleep and started getting headaches every day because of it, but he said he could not afford one. However, soon after he refused buying me an alarm clock, he bought a bike worth a hundred rupees for his 6-year-old brother, Gajinder. That made my heart ache so much. He could not even spend ten rupees to buy me a clock when I was barely getting any sleep at night.

CHAPTER 7

Sanjeev had started his engineering degree and was taking night classes. He would come home at 9:00 p.m. and go straight to see his father and brothers, who lived on the first floor, and spend time talking to them. I always had to wait for him until he came up at 11:00 p.m. and then make fresh roti's and serve his dinner. I then had to clean up, wash the dishes and massage his feet until 1:30 a.m. when he would eventually go to sleep. We slept on the floor as we did not have a bed. But whatever I felt, I had no power to say it. If I ever voiced my opinion, Sanjeev would slap my head and tell me to ask my father for anything.

He was still very angry that my father did not give him any dowry, so he would constantly talk about wanting to marry another girl. Her name was Vimla. She had attended the same university as Sanjeev and was studying to be a doctor. Sanjeev was very interested in Vimla but she did not feel the same about him, so he thought that after he finished his electrical engineering degree, she might agree to marry him. Sanjeev had a cousin called Gulab who came over for breakfast every weekend and knew the right things to say to Sanjeev to make him feel happy. He would tell Sanjeev whatever he wanted to hear, and they would both openly make plans to kidnap Vimla and bring her to Sanjeev, so he could marry her. Sanjeev did not care what was happening to my feelings. I waited on him hand and foot, yet he was making plans to marry someone else right in front of me. No woman wants to hear that from the man she just married. However, Sanjeev didn't care what he was doing to me because he never loved me.

Sanjeev would often say that my father sold me to him instead of giving him dowry money. When he went shopping with me, he would tell all the shop keepers that my father did not feed me and that I was just sold to him. I would get so humiliated, but Sanjeev did not care if he shamed me because he had no respect for me. Whenever we went out, he always found reasons to argue with me or criticize me. He would say that I walked funny and that I didn't bend my knees when I walked or would ask me why I walk at the edge of the curb, or why I was walking on the other side of the curb, or why I walked straight and not with my head down. There was always something I was doing wrong in his eyes. He would keep on ranting the whole time until we got back home. He talked so much that sometimes people looked at him strangely because they thought he was talking to himself because I did not say anything back to him.

Sanjeev's personality was so unpleasant that even his parents and all his brothers hated him for it. His own mother said that he was dead to her, his father cursed him day and night, and all his siblings called him mental. He may have loved his brothers and worried about them and their education, but he would hit and push them too hard to pressure them to get a degree. They were not interested and just hated him more for that. He also could not hold a job for more than six months at a time as he could never get along with his colleagues. I heard that in his very first job, Sanjeev had gotten into an argument with a colleague and wound up slapping him, so he was let go.

Sanjeev's parents only put up with him because he was the family's main source of income. His mother used to say they worked hard to give Sanjeev an education, so he could earn money and look after all his siblings. Sanjeev's father was not a very nice person either. He was very demanding and would insist that Sanjeev give him all his pay. This in turn led to Sanjeev not having anything left for himself, and perhaps caused his anger and rude behavior. I was living in an extremely hateful family. Brothers hating brothers, parents hating Sanjeev, and Sanjeev hating me.

Soon, I got pregnant with my first child, but that did not change anything. I was still not getting enough sleep after doing everyone's cooking, laundry, ironing and cleaning, so I started having regular migraines. Sanjeev did not make it any easier for me either. Being pregnant, I was throwing up every day, in addition to the headaches and exhaustion. Once, Govind had asked Sanjeev to stop nagging me because I had a migraine, but all Sanjeev could say, unsympathetically, was "What's so new, she has a headache every day, what do you want me to do?"

I was only in Delhi for six months and was 3 months pregnant before Sanjeev dropped me off at his mother's house in the village to help her and they took Govind's wife to help in Delhi. It did not matter to them if a woman was pregnant, sick, a child or old; if she lived in her in-law's house, she was forced to do all the housework for every member of the family. It was very difficult for me and became even harder as I ended up doing more work than ever in the village while I was pregnant.

Sanjeev's sister, Meena, lived in the village with their mother even though she had already been married to a college professor. Her husband did not want to take her to Delhi because she was uneducated and did not know how to communicate with his friends. He wanted to leave her with his mother, but she wanted to live with her own mother instead. My mother-in-law was happy to keep her around because she would get help from her to do the housework before I had arrived.

While I was in the village, my routine was to wake up very early in the mornings to grind wheat flour and walk a long distance to the other village to bring water from their water-well for drinking and cooking. The water-well in our village produced salty water which we could only use to wash dishes, clothes, and ourselves. I then had to make breakfast for Gajinder and Mahesh, Sanjeev's youngest siblings, who were 6 and 4 years old. I also had to get them ready for school, since they could barely dress themselves. After that, I cleaned the dishes, swept the floor and washed everyone's clothes. By the time I was finished with all that, it was time to make lunch. My mother-in-law and sister in-law went to the fields in the mornings for a couple of hours to dig the grass for the cow and buffalo they had. When they came home, they expected lunch to be served immediately. I worked as fast as I could but sometimes, if I was a bit late in making lunch, Meena would shout at me and ask me what I had been doing all day. She was a nightmare; her voice was so harsh that she could make a mountain cry. I never answered back. Every time she shouted at me, I would just go to my room and wipe my tears away before returning to finish doing the housework. Meena wanted to give me more work by having me go with her to dig the grass but realized she could not do so as no one would be left to do the housework.

Meanwhile, my mother-in-law complained and would say "What do I do all day that I can't comb my hair as I look like a road sweeper with unkempt hair". She only cared about the way I looked because she was worried what the neighbours would say. She did not want to acknowledge the list of chores they would give me before leaving each day that I had to make sure was done before they arrived back. While my mother-in-law nitpicked on my hair, all I had on my mind was what work I had to do next. Every night, I was also forced to massage my mother-in-law's legs because she said they were hurting, and by the time I finished, I was so tired and sleepy that when I hit the pillow, I had no idea in the morning if I had even gone to sleep which was not good for me being pregnant.

Sanjeev used to visit every other weekend from the city. All I heard while he was around was his mother complaining about me, saying that I was not capable of doing anything. He always took his mother's side and would say "yes mother, she's like that" or "yes, she doesn't know anything". This encouraged his brother Govind and Mohan to become horrible to me too, as no one showed any care or respect for me. They felt entitled to treat me the way they wanted. I felt like an abused servant. Once Mohan brought shit on a stick and tried to force me to eat it, but when I refused, he started insulting me. They enjoyed taunting me and making me feel worse than I already felt. Mohan even said that ever since I came along, their family had been destroyed and that I was the reason they were poor. They continued to say horrible things to hurt me, but I did not say anything back to defend myself.

I continued working while being subjected to cruel treatment and unhappiness even when my daughter, Kajal, was born in 1958. The day she was born, my mother-in-law told the mid-wife to kick me between the legs. I asked why, and my mother-in-law said it was to keep my uterus in. Soon after the midwife left, Meena gave me a week-old, dried-up roti and told me to eat it to stop the pain after child birth. I believed her and ate it, but as soon as I finished, I had such severe stomach pains which were really unbearable. My mother-in-law waited until the evening, when she called over an old man from the village who was known to take bad spirits away. He told me that I was possessed with a ghost, so he splashed some water on me and started shaking a broom all over me in an attempt to rid me of the pain. It did not help. All day and night, I cried with excruciating stomach pains until the next day, when I did feel better. A few days later, Govind came to the village. When he saw Kajal, he picked her up and put her face towards the sun to try and force her to look at it, as he wanted her to go blind. Luckily, Kajal automatically closed her eyes very tightly. All his mother did was laugh it off while telling her son not to do that.

Usually in India, women are expected to rest for 40 days after giving birth, however there was no luck for me. Sanjeev's family needed someone to do all the housework, so I was back in the kitchen after only 10 days. Sanjeev came after a few weeks to visit us in the village. He was very disappointed because he was expecting a boy and he did not even want to look at or hold his daughter. Once when Kajal was crying and I was busy, I asked Sanjeev to hold her for a few minutes. But when he did hold her, and she did not stop crying, he threw her on the bed while he was standing, so after that day, I never asked him again. He never bothered to hide his displeasure either, and whenever he saw a woman who had a baby boy, he always pointed out how lucky she was.

When our daughter was 6 months old, Sanjeev came to take us from the village to Delhi and Govind's wife went to the village. My father-in-law had made arrangements that Govind's wife, Durga, and I, alternate living in the village for 6 months and in Delhi for 6 months. However, she was never treated the way I was because she had the support of her husband. Because Sanjeev was so mean and brutal to everyone, no one liked him, so they took their hatred out on me. This didn't affect him at all, but it caused me so much hurt and pain instead.

CHAPTER 8

While I was in Delhi, I found out that both Meena and my mother-in-law had been pregnant and were both about to give birth. I returned to the village after 6 months in Delhi, and by that time, they both had 6-month-old babies. Meena had a son and my mother-in-law had a daughter she named Tanuja. I was now back in the village doing all the same work as before, in addition to looking after 3 babies, only one of which was mine.

Before Meena and her mother went out to the fields, they ordered me to make lunch, do all the chores and make sure the babies did not cry. Kajal was 1-year-old and their babies were both 6 months, so when the babies would cry, I could either comfort them and not do the housework, or work and let them cry for a bit. I worked as fast as I possibly could while I also tried to care for the babies and stop them from crying, but it was impossible to do it all by myself. One of the neighbors complained about me to my mother-in-law and said that I made the children cry all the time, each day. It was hard listening to their complaints when I was trying so hard to do my best.

Govind's wife came to the village to have her first child there. After she gave birth to a baby boy, I asked her if she had eaten a one-week old, dry roti and if the midwife had kicked her between her legs. She said "No" and laughed. She asked me why a midwife would do that. I realized in that moment, that my mother-in-law did all these things to me because she hoped that I would die. She had only brought the old man from the village to witness my death caused by stomach pain. She planned it so that she could get money regularly from Sanjeev for our daughter, Kajal. She knew he would never keep Kajal with him, but he would still provide for her needs. I couldn't even imagine how they would have treated her if I wasn't alive. My mother-in-law must have been very disappointed when I did not die.

I was doing so much work without rest or nutrition, that I lost a lot of weight. I became weak and anemic to the point that other villagers would mention it. Kajal also got really sick to the point where she could not even take any medication as it would come out immediately at the other end. She had become so weak that I could not even hear her cry in the same room. She looked almost like a skeleton, you could count each of her bones protruding from her little body. My mother-in-law did not want to keep us around because she did not want the responsibility of taking care of us. She also cared even less for us because Sanjeev had stopped sending money to her after getting fired from his job. I did not know until later that she had sent Meena to my father to tell him that we were so sick that we might not make it. She told him that if he wanted to see us he should call us there. My father sent my brother to bring us to Delhi, so that both Kajal and I could receive medical treatment.

When my father saw me, he said I looked like a skeleton and he was ashamed what the neighbours would say if they saw me that way together with my ripped clothes. He told me not to go onto the balcony until he bought new clothes for me, just in case someone saw me. In return, both my father and brother nagged me every day that I married a useless man, who had no manners, could not even hold a job, and for this reason I would be forced to beg for the rest of my life. My father would default to one of his favorite statements, that a married woman should not stay at her father's house. As usual, I listened in silence while thinking that he should never have let me marry Sanjeev in the first place.

My father always hated Sanjeev, which I could understand. But because of that, he did not like my children either, and that hurt me a lot. I know how loving he was to my sisters' children. He would play with them, talk to them and show them many places because he liked my rich brother-in-law and my sister better. I felt pressured living there because I knew I was a burden to my father. I don't remember how long we stayed at my father's house, but when Kajal and I started getting better, I asked Sanjeev to take us with him every time he visited. After all, he only lived a few streets away, and if I had to pick one person's insults to take then I would rather take his.

When Sanjeev found another job, he rented his cousin-sister's house who had subleased it to us at a higher rent than they were paying themselves. It was the same cousin that Sanjeev's mother hated, and the same house that my mother-in-law had brought me to, where he had shouted at me to leave as he was divorcing me. After Sanjeev moved in he picked Kajal and me up from my father's house and brought us there. Although it was a two-bedroom house, only one bedroom was available because the other one was being used by Sanjeev's cousin as storage. While we were living there, I became pregnant soon after with my second child.

While we were renting the house, Sanjeev spent all his time with his cousin-sister who had moved to another apartment close by, as he felt obligated to see her since she was renting us her house. Meanwhile, her husband would come to our house because he knew I was alone. He pretended to get something from the storage room but in reality, he was constantly staring at me. It felt very scary and intimidating but when I told Sanjeev, he just laughed it off. But, when I told the woman, who lived next door about it, she made sure she was always there with me every time he came. She also never liked Sanjeev's cousin and her husband while they were her neighbours as they used to argue a lot. He came a few times but when he could not get me alone, he became frustrated. He told his wife that their things were missing from the room and Sanjeev immediately said that I must be the one taking their belongings to put me down as usual. I was hurt, but I could not say anything to him as there was no point. I did, however, ask him if we could move to another rented house but he refused.

CHAPTER 9

The wives of Sanjeev's friends were all educated and could speak English. That was why he never took me to their homes for get-togethers or parties. However, when he talked badly about me to his friends they found it rude and mean-spirited. They were surprised at how he could criticize me like that. So, one by one, Sanjeev's friends began disconnecting from him until he had none left. His parents and siblings also had been disengaged from him for a long time. I was the only one unable to leave him due to my circumstances. My father did not want anything to do with me because as far as he was concerned, it was my idea to marry Sanjeev and therefore my circumstances to deal with. My brother always accused me of killing our mother and younger brother just to hurt me, and my sister was married and living with her husband. I was stuck with Sanjeev for better or for worse. In my case it was all for worse and nothing else.

Soon after, in 1959, I gave birth to my second child in Delhi. He was a baby boy we named Arjun. When Arjun was only a few months old, Sanjeev told me to go to high school because he wanted me to speak in English like his friends' wives. It was difficult for me because I had two very young children and all of Sanjeev's family members to look after. I had also become very weak because I did not have any nutritious food before or after childbirth. Sanjeev brought his sister, Meena, and her son, so that she could look after our 2 young children while I attended school. But, the main reason Meena wanted to come to Delhi was to receive treatment as she was sick for a long time in the village. She had spots all over her lower body and would constantly throw up after eating. Instead of having her help with watching over my children, I ended up cleaning her vomit every day and looking after her and her son who was younger than Kajal. It was very difficult for me to bare this added responsibility while I was trying to take care of my own family and going to school at the same time.

I had nothing left in me and felt totally worn out. Soon enough, Meena fully recovered and went back to the village. Sanjeev continued to spend all his time, day and night, with his cousin-sister. He left me and the children in the sweltering heat while he slept in the open air of his cousin-sister's house. I was so frustrated and pained this one day, that I finally said to Sanjeev that he might as well be married to her if that's where he preferred to spend his time. One of the neighbour's overheard me and told his cousin-sister. She then came over to the house and said she was going to lock the second bedroom and I said if that was the case, then we should give only half the rent. She got even madder at me. Sanjeev also got angry at me for talking to her like that, so he hit me. I said I would find another house to rent to which he simply replied, go ahead.

With the help of the same lady next door, I found a two-bedroom house close by. It was bigger than the house we had been staying in and also had a bigger living room. I moved to the new place within the day with the help of some neighbourhood girls. It was quite easy to move as we did not have any furniture of our own, so the only things we had to move were the few clothes and dishes we had. Once I had moved everything over, I told Sanjeev that he could come straight there. He was happy to leave as the place I had found was cheaper to rent. His cousin-sister and her husband became upset as they would be losing their rental income from us.

Meanwhile I was getting sicker and started developing all of Meena's symptoms. The bigger problem was that I still had to continue going to school. It got so bad that I was only able to do half of my exams, and Sanjeev did not even notice how sick I was. He did not care that I could not even walk anymore and had to do all the work crawling from one room to the other. It wasn't until the neighbours started saying that I had TB and they did not want me around their family that he had no choice but to take me to the hospital where I had x-rays and several tests taken. I was eighteen years old and my weight was only 60 lbs, so the doctor asked Sanjeev to take me to a specialist. We went there with Kajal and Arjun as no one else could take care of them that day. But when the doctor saw me holding my son, he immediately got very angry at Sanjeev and crossly told him to take the child away from me. He said that he should have more sense as I was clearly too weak to be looking after a child, and he pointed out that Sanjeev was so much older than I was and should be more understanding. The specialist confirmed that I did not have TB and also told me to come to the hospital twice a week to administer a dozen injections to get better. He said because I was so weak and anemic I needed good nutrition. It was true that I was not eating enough nutritious food such as vegetables and fruits, because Sanjeev would finish anything I cooked and any food that he would ever bring home. After he finished eating, he would always tell me that he would bring fruits and vegetables for me later, but he never did.

I got a lot better with the injections, but it was hard to get back to full health as I was not given the opportunity to rest as I had to continue to do all the chores irrespective of how I was feeling. It was at this time that Sanjeev wanted Arjun's first hair cut at the temple in the village. His cousin's wife and her friend came with us. They were both staying at his cousins' house, while I went with our children and Sanjeev to my mother-in-law's house. Govind was there and as soon as he saw me he grabbed both my hands forcefully and started pushing me out of the house and said I had no right being there. I have no idea why he said and did that. I was wearing new glass bangles that I had just bought. Govind broke all my bangles cutting both my wrists, as he pushed me out. Meanwhile, Sanjeev was standing outside the door, simply watching everything happen. When I saw him, I was hoping he would come to my rescue, but he never came nor said anything to Govind. I walked with tears in my eyes and pain deep in my heart as we walked to the temple. When we got there Sanjeev's cousin's wife and her friend were already there. When they saw how I looked with dried tears around my eyes, both my wrists bruised and scratched, and all my bangles gone, they both looked very sorry for me, yet neither of them asked me about it. The next day, we returned to Delhi and I asked Sanjeev why he watched Govind drag me out of the house and did not come to stop his brother. All he could say was that I wouldn't understand his situation. When I asked what situation he was referring to, he would say, as per usual, "If you don't know, how can I tell you", or, "Why should I tell you".

Soon after my treatment, Sanjeev found out he was being transferred to Jammu Kashmir. He was working as an Engineer in *All India Radio*. He dropped us back to my father's house and told my father he would call us as soon as he finds a place where we can all stay.

Around two months later, Sanjeev had settled in his job and he called us to Jammu Kashmir. My father put us on the train and I was happy to leave his place. The seating on the long-distance night trains were made of compartments with two benches facing opposite each other. I had taken up one side of the bench as both my children were sleeping. When the train reached the next station, it had started to get full. A rough looking man came into the compartment I was in and angrily told me to move when he saw that I was sitting alone with my sleeping children. However, a man who was sitting opposite me told him off by saying "Can't you see the children are sleeping" and he made some space for the man to sit beside him. Although I felt very grateful towards the man for sticking up for me, I could not get the words out to thank him. Speaking out had become an ingrown fear which prevented me from saying anything at all. I sometimes still wish I had the courage to have thanked him for his support at that time.

Sanjeev picked us up from the station in a Rickshaw. I don't recall exactly how I felt in that moment, but I was surely relieved to be with Sanjeev despite how he was, instead of being with my father. The house had three floors; the landlord lived on the main floor and we were one of two lodgers on the second floor. The room we had was quite large with a walk-in storage and a small kitchen. However, there was only one small bathroom between us and the other lodger that we both shared and where we had to also bathe and wash our clothing. There were two toilets on the third floor which everyone had to use including the landlord as well as the other lodger living on the third floor.

I was still very weak, so I went to see a doctor in Jammu Kashmir. She gave some medication and also told me that I should not have any more children for a while. She gave me contraceptives to use but Sanjeev said doctors didn't know anything and he threw all the contraceptives away. As soon as I was a little bit better I got pregnant again. It made me so weak that as soon as I went to bed, I felt as if my head was sinking deeper and deeper. Once or twice Sanjeev thought I was dead. He asked if I had fainted, yet when I told him how I felt when I went to sleep, he still did not bother to take me to the doctor for a checkup, so I forced myself to go alone because I was pregnant. The doctor gave me an injection and asked me to come twice a week to get further injections for several weeks to help me get better. Nine months later, in 1961, I had another daughter, Asha. I was later to find out about Asha's condition which I now believe could have been due to either my severe weakness or the number of injections I was having for my treatment which the doctors did not know or consider the impact at that time on the effect it could have on an unborn child.

I found out that all my neighbours had been betting that at childbirth I would die. For me, there was no such luck! Sanjeev then started cursing our son that he brought a girl, because an old Indian saying states that the older child brings the next one. Because of that, Sanjeev believed that our son wanted a sister. I cannot even describe how many insulting names Sanjeev was calling me during that time because I had a second daughter. He then started eating out every day and justified it by saying my hands are not clean for at least 40 days after child birth. But the truth is, women are supposed to rest for 40 days after child birth and has nothing to do with unclean hands. He just made it up to suit himself as he did not want to help me; instead he told me to cook for the children and myself while he ate out. His unkind words added salt on my already wounded and burning heart about his lack of care for us.

He also continually lusted after other women, but they never gave him a second look. He was physically unfit, weighing almost 300 lbs at 5' 3" with an immature attitude. But he thought he had everything going for him because he was an engineer.

Once Arjun and Kajal were playing and chasing each other in the other room while I was cooking in the kitchen. As soon as I finished making paratha and put the greasy frying pan aside on the floor, Arjun came running into the kitchen really fast and fell suddenly onto the hot frying pan. Arjun was only two years old and got burnt really badly on one side of his bum. As soon as Sanjeev came home I told him that we should quickly take him to the hospital for treatment. He refused and said he did not believe in doctors and when I opened my mouth to try to persuade him that Arjun was in so much pain, he got really angry at me and said I burnt him. It was very hard hearing his cold and insensitive words accusing me and his lack of care about the pain Arjun was feeling. I felt so wounded and powerless. I was also still quite weak after giving birth to Asha and was unable to hold or carry both Asha, who was just two weeks old and Arjun to walk all the way to the hospital as I could not pay for a Rickshaw as I had absolutely no money. I had even thought of borrowing some money from the neighbours, but I was terrified by Sanjeev and did not dare to do anything without his permission. One day our landlady asked me why I was not taking Arjun to the hospital as she could obviously see he was in so much pain. When I told her that Sanjeev does not believe in doctors, she went to him and insisted he take Arjun to get treated as he was evidently not getting better at home and was actually getting worse. Sanjeev finally accepted it and we took Arjun to the hospital where the doctor admitted him immediately. Asha and I stayed with Arjun at the hospital with just one thin bed sheet we had taken with us. It was winter months and the hospital was very cold. They did not provide anything for parents while they stayed at the hospital with their child. We had to sleep on the floor with the thin bed sheet I had bought. I put Asha on my chest to keep her warm, but I shivered all night on the cold cement floor for two weeks until Arjun got better.

When we came back home from the hospital, I asked Sanjeev where Kajal was. He said he is going to bring her as she was staying at his friend's house. Kajal was just 4 years old and Sanjeev could not even look after her for 2 weeks. He brought her home looking as if she came from the streets. She did not have a bath; her face was very dirty, and she was wearing the same dress for two weeks. It was sad to see her that way, so I mentioned to Sanjeev that they could have at least washed her face. Instead of acknowledging the fact, he got really mad with me and angrily said I should be more grateful to them as they kept her for 2 weeks. He then walked away to eat out and left me alone with the 3 children on the day we arrived back from the hospital. There was nothing to eat at home, so with the very little supply we had I made something for the children and myself to eat.

When Asha was a few weeks old, she was very constipated and only passed stool every eight days. I was still very naïve at that time and happily said that my daughter was so clean, she did not pass stool every day. No one told me that it was actually bad to have a child so constipated. When she was one month old she started having seizures. When the seizures happened, there would be 4 in a day, approximately 4 hours apart. I took Asha to the hospital where the doctor provided medicine for the constipation, but nothing for her seizure. The medicine didn't work as she continued to be either constipated or get diarrhea. And the seizures continued.

I was so worried about Asha being sick all the time, so I took her to the hospital often and left my two young children, Kajal and Arjun, with the neighbor's children to play. Sanjeev didn't even care and would hang around with his friends after work. He was in his own world and I was in mine. On one of our hospital visits, Asha had a seizure right in front of the doctor, but he did not do anything. He just sent us back home and said that everything was fine. When Asha was 3 years old I took her to a different doctor as she was not getting better. Apart from the seizures, she was not saying any age appropriate words, which I found worrying. But again, the doctor was rude and just said "She will talk!!" The doctor even asked me sarcastically "Do you think that she will talk in one day!?" Still her seizures were not addressed. After that I stopped asking doctors altogether. Sanjeev was heartless and would often say "when is she going to die" whenever he would see her. I asked people what I could possibly do. I tried every suggestion they provided and prayed to God that she would get better, but nothing helped. When people started calling her mental, I realized that there was something to it. The seizures had caused her to actually become developmentally delayed and affected her ability to speak.

We lived in Jammu Kashmir for two years until Sanjeev got fired from his job again. He brought us back to his mother's house in the village while he went back to Delhi to look for a job. There I was again, now with three children of my own, being moved around from one house to another, unwanted in all of them. His sister, Meena and her two children still lived there. Meena not only shouted at me but also harshly snapped at my children and made them cry.

A few months later, Sanjeev found a job in Madras and I found out I was pregnant with my fourth child. Mohan's wife Ramrati was also in the village at that time. She was not a nice person, but Sanjeev liked her and always praised her. Once I watched Sanjeev tailing behind her to her room and when I asked Sanjeev about it, he said that he thought he was following me. Ramrati knew that Sanjeev liked her. She was very proud of herself and did not care about me or my children and was quite mean. Once she burnt my son's hand with hot water and told me it was by accident. She then blamed my son that he put his hand in the hot water, and it was his fault.

When I gave birth to my daughter, Anjali, in 1964, Ramrati left the next day. She went to her parent's house to ensure she did not have to cook or do any housework as I had been doing it all up until the day I gave birth. This meant I was back doing all the chores after only 10 days instead of the usual 40 days that women were expected to rest and take care of their baby after giving birth. Sanjeev was once again disappointed for another girl. He also lost his job soon after, so he came to see us in the village for a few days before he went back to Delhi to stay with his father while he tried to find a job.

Around six months later Sanjeev got a really good paying job in Sindri near Calcutta, which included a company house. He would send 300 rupees a month which was a lot of money at that time to his mother in the village. Because of that she did not want me to join him in Sindri so that she could continue receiving regular money from him. He was also sending money to Gajinder for his studies at the college in Delhi. I did not get a penny of his money but had to continue to do all the housework as an unpaid worker. They would eat roti that I made for them with milk and yogurt whereas my children and I had to eat the roti with pickles only. As Sanjeev had no feelings for me, he also ignored the children and did not even notice how skinny and deprived we all were. Once when my mother-in-law said I eat too much, and that Sanjeev did not send enough money to feed me or my children, I mentioned that he sends 300 rupees a month and that should be more than enough. She got really angry with me and told me that I would have to cook separately from now on. She then dumped a bag of wheat in front of me which had been thrown away a long time ago. When I started grinding them, there was no flour but just ground shells. They had been eaten by brown insects we called Surarri. I then had to go outside the village with my son where there were lots of trees so that I could get wood pieces to cook with. When I put the ground shells into the boiling water all the brown insects floated up. I had to take all the dead floating insects out of the saucepan to make the rest as a salty porridge, so my children and I could have something to eat. It was a very difficult time for us.

Govind would come to see his mother regularly, spending two weeks at a time and adding further pain and misery to what I was already going through. He was so angry at Sanjeev that he continually took his revenge out on me and my children instead. Wherever and whenever Govind would find an opportunity to inflict pain he relished in it. Even when I used to grind the wheat for them, he would take a piece out of the hand-grinding machine, so it would make it extremely difficult for me to move it and consequently take all my energy and strength to grind it into flour. When I would ask him to put the piece back into the machine, he would laugh and mockingly ridicule me to his mother and sister how I talk and complain like "Delhi people". Once he was pretending to be a joker but intentionally hit my nose so hard with his fist that it hurt me severely for years and caused breathing problems which I still have to this day on one side of my nostril. I was constantly subjected to cruelty in some form or another by Sanjeev's family and they all continually punished me and my children every way they possibly could. Once Tanuja threw a few hot coals on Anjali's back and burning her permanently. When I asked her why she had done it, she just laughed and said she was just playing. Another time was when Gajinder, Mahesh and Tanuja were all on the roof top and one of them pushed Kajal down. It took days for her to recover. The only saving grace was the fact she had fallen on soft ground that prevented her from a severe or permanent injury. They would also slap my children around constantly for absolutely no reason to make them cry and feel miserable.

When Sanjeev would come to visit he would bring lots of school supplies which were very hard to get in the village and ask Mahesh to share it with everyone. However, Mahesh would lock it up in the cupboard and refused to give it to Arjun and Kajal for their school work. He would make them beg and beg before he finally gave them a small supply which would barely last them, so they would have to constantly beg him again. Even daily events were made tortuous. When I used to comb my children's hair, Tanuja would later hide the brush, so I would not be able to comb their hair and have to send them to school in that way. I was seeing my children suffer as I was suffering myself and it was very hard for me to endure. Living a day without some form of torment or abuse was so few and far between that it was making it extremely difficult for me to cope with.

Day after day, the constant torment spiraled me into deeper depression. The sadness and pain drenched every part of me, making it impossible for any hopes of living. I would go to bed every night planning to kill myself with my children as I did not want to leave them to suffer in the hands of Sanjeev's family. I heard that there was a pond in the village so deep even elephants can drown. Sometimes I thought that I would not take my son with me because I knew Sanjeev would take care of him because he is a boy. But Sanjeev would never care for our daughters and would just leave them behind in the village to slave for his mother and the rest of his family. I thought and made plans all night long but, in the morning, I woke up to all the usual responsibilities that I was burdened with and started my day the same way again. We lived in the village under these grueling conditions for more than a year before Sanjeev was forced to take us with him to Sindri when Arjun and I had become too sick. His family did not want to take care of us nor spend a penny on our medical treatment.

CHAPTER 10

While I was coping with my real life, bearing children and dealing with all the situations during the day, I would escape into my pretend life at night. In my pretend life, Vikram and Kamla adopted us. They were well established and modern. We called them mommy and papa. In this life I attended private school, like I always wanted. My brother Danny was very wise and wanted me to have a good education. I learned everything from music, dance and singing. In this life, I was good at everything I touched or did. Mommy and Papa called me their golden girl. I also started swimming and became a champion in their eyes. At the back of my mind, I considered this to be my real life.

Here I was gifted, finished my high school and started University doing a Law Degree. My adoptive parents and my brother came to see me almost every weekend. All the boys were after me and all the girls were very jealous, but I was not interested with the boys and kept them away. I knew what kind of boy I wanted to marry. He had to be very special, who would have eyes for me only and nobody else and I knew I would know at first sight.

I had one childhood best friend, Maya, who lived next door. We both attended the same University and wherever we went, we went together. One day in my second year at University, Maya was feeling ill, so I had to go to lunch by myself. After lunch, I went to get myself a coffee, but as I took my coffee and turned around, I bumped into a boy and spilt it all over his shirt. I apologized, and he said in a sweet voice "No harm done". Then I looked up at his face and saw how handsome he was, as if he came from another world. I offered to dry clean his shirt, but he refused, so I said at least let me buy you a coffee. He agreed. I bought two coffees and we sat at the same table and we both introduced ourselves. He said his name was Raj and he was doing a medical degree. I could not believe how handsome and polite he was. I could feel that he was thinking the same of me. Then I looked around and saw everyone looking at us. Some boys said loudly "how come she never let us come near her and she is talking to him so long". We both ignored them. After that day, Raj started coming every lunch time to spend time with me. Slowly we started falling in love with each other.

When Maya came back, I introduced Raj to her. She liked him and said what a lucky girl I was. I was so happy to hear that. My thoughts then went to my brother Danny. I always shared everything with him and always took his advice, but I was worried whether Danny would like Raj or not. I respected and cared about Danny's opinion as he was everything to me. He was the one who took care of me and comforted me through my awful childhood. He was like a parent to me and I would never forget that, so I really needed his approval to marry Raj. I had already given my heart to Raj so in my mind, I decided I would not marry anyone else if I could not marry Raj.

When I went home on summer vacation, my parents and Danny were happy to see me, including Ramu Kaka, our housekeeper who I always missed when I was away from home. I was avoiding Danny, but he always knew when I had something on my mind, so he asked me to come for a drive with him. He drove some distance and then stopped the car in a quiet place and then asked me what was bothering me. I told him about Raj. Danny said that he trusted my judgment, as he knew that I could see through people, but he still wanted to know more about Raj. I told him that Raj was doing medicine and was living with his parents and one younger brother called Harry. Raj also had an older sister, Suroj, who was married to a doctor. They had two children, a boy and girl. I felt relieved after talking with Danny and knew that it would now be easy to introduce Raj to Mommy and Papa - especially Papa as he was very easy going and, in his eyes, I could never do anything wrong.

Raj and I would phone each other over the summer holidays. He would tell me that his brother Harry had not done well at High School because he just wanted to have fun and go out with girls. Their parents were not happy with him, but Harry did not care. Before I went back to university, my family invited Raj and his family for dinner. As soon as my family saw Raj, they liked him immediately. Raj's parents also said they could not wait to meet me after they saw my photo and heard all about me from Raj.

CHAPTER 11

Back in the village in my real life, before Sanjeev picked us up, I had started getting spots all over my face because of the extreme heat and dust. For the same reasons my son started having really bad eye problems. My mother-in-law once again did not want to spend any money on my son's eye treatment or on mine. She also continued to state we ate too much, and that Sanjeev did not send enough money to keep us there. However, while we were living there she did not give me or my children any vegetables or fruits or even milk although she had a cow and buffalo. She preferred to give the milk and lassi to her neighbours rather than us. It wasn't until my father-in-law came to see his children and saw how bad my son's eyes were that he wrote to Sanjeev to take us back with him to Sindri. Finally, Sanjeev came and took us with him after having left us in the village for over a year.

In Sindri he lived in the area where there were only company bungalows, and everyone knew each other. He felt ashamed of how we looked so he first took us to his friend's house in a different city for a few days hoping that we would heal. Obviously without any treatment we could not get better, so he had to eventually bring us to his house. There we saw a doctor in the hospital who prescribed medication and creams for our son and me.

When Anjali was only 6 months old I got pregnant with my 5th child. It was difficult for me as Sanjeev would not let me use any protection. He criticized every new kind that came out and said so many women had tried them, and something always went wrong. But the reason he said all those things was because he wanted to have another son. In that small colony where we lived no one had more than 2 children. Everywhere we went, people laughed at us and counted the number of children we had. Sanjeev started feeling a little ashamed for the first time, so he finally told me to ask the doctor for a hysterectomy after childbirth. The doctor refused because I was too weak and suggested that Sanjeev should get a vasectomy instead. Sanjeev did not like what he heard, but he had no choice. The doctor refused to do any surgery on me, so he could not force me and therefore had to get a vasectomy done himself.

Sanjeev used to only call his mother, mainly to update her about where he lived and worked. However, when I was pregnant with my 5th child, he asked her to come and help. When she came with her youngest daughter, Tanuja, I noticed she had a big knot in the corner of her sari. So many times, I wanted to see what she was hiding there, but every time she changed, she made sure she hid the thing in the new sari she was wearing.

The day my daughter, Tara, was born in 1965, my mother-in-law brought me cold milk (not even warmed) and nothing else, even though she knew the hospitals in India did not provide any food. I soon found out from my mother-in-law that when Sanjeev heard I had a 4th daughter, he got so mad that he punched Anjali who was only 15 months old so hard that she could not breathe for a few minutes. He shouted and cursed at her for bringing a girl after her. I fell into a deeper depression then. Here I was left all alone at the hospital with no food and only cold milk and no one caring about me. In my hurt, pain and loneliness I hid my face in the hospital blanket and started crying all day. I heard some women whispering to each other about me crying all the time, but no one came to ask me why. All I did was cry then and did not feel like talking to anyone, including my children. No one knew how sad I was. I did not know about depression then, and only learned about it much later in my life.

About 2 months later, my mother-in-law managed to persuade Sanjeev to send me and the children back to the village with her, so I could continue to do her housework and that way she could also receive money from Sanjeev. When we were back in the village I also found out the secret of what my mother-in-law had been hiding in her sari knot. It was when a woman came to see my mother-in-law to ask her if that thing had worked on me. My mother-in-law was so busy arguing with her that she did not notice I was listening. She screamed at the woman that it did not work on me. I can't remember after so many years what exactly was said but I know the overwhelming feeling that took over my whole body when I found out that my mother in law was still trying to kill me after having five children. I was totally shocked and shattered that I wanted to tell her right there and then to kill me to satisfy herself. But it was the fear of leaving my children motherless to a vulnerable life riddled with pain and sorrow that I did not ever want them to be subjected to, as I was, without my mother, so I remained in silence.

I was once again slaving away for Sanjeev's family while looking after their children as well as trying to look after my own. In addition, my mother-in-law burdened me with further work, by forcing me to sew all the neighbour's clothes, while she took their money. I ended up working every evening, right after all my day time chores, late into the night, using the dim light of the oil lantern. That is when my eyes started getting really bad and I eventually was unable to sew any longer and had to start refusing.

Sanjeev was sending money for Gajinder's education and also had a larger rent to pay in Sindri, so he was unable to send too much money to his mother. Sanjeev's parents were not happy about that, so my father-in-law wrote to Sanjeev and told him to take us back. We were in the village for around 6 months before Sanjeev came to take us with him to Sindri.

CHAPTER 12

At night, whenever I went into my pretend life I would find happiness, peace and serenity that I was missing in my real life. I could be whatever I wanted, and it felt wonderful. If I hadn't had this pretend life I think I would have truly gone crazy a long time ago.

I had a vision in my pretend life that I was going to win the lottery, so when I finished university, I bought a ticket with the intention of giving my winnings to my parents. I actually did win the lottery this time, so I gave my winnings to them to acknowledge the love and support they had given Danny and me. Our adoptive parents, Vikram and Kamla did not want to take it though. I really had to insist, saying that if they loved me enough they should take it. After a lot of persuasion, they finally gave in.

My papa then decided to buy a big plot of land with the lottery money. On it he wanted to build exactly two houses, three stories high with a basement, one for me and one for Danny. The land was so big that he also decided to build a tennis court and swimming pool between the houses. He also made a room for a guard outside the entrance. I was very happy to see the two identical houses side by side. Both looked amazingly beautiful. It was especially important to me that my brother lived next door to me. He protected me so much, like the roof that protects the house and everybody in it.

In this pretend life, I finished my law degree and Raj was already doing a PhD in medicine. While he was busy with his post-graduate, I also started a PhD in Defense Law. When Raj and I finished our education, papa and Danny started my wedding plans. Money was no object, so they asked if I wanted to add any special wish for my wedding. I said I wanted to go on an elephant the first time I went to my husband's house and I also wanted Scottish bag-pipes for the wedding music. They liked my choices and were happy to arrange that for me. I felt very lucky that both my future life partner and his family were such nice people. I could not have asked for anyone nicer than them. I also felt free to talk with them openly and about everything. My life was very good.

In my pretend life, I got married and after all the goodbyes, I left with my husband on an elephant. We started the wedding procession to my in-law's house. My father-in-law was throwing a lot of money up in the air as customary, and a lot of people were dancing, including my brothers-in-law, to all the music and bagpipes. To keep the crowd away, my father hired a lot of police to control them. As Raj and I went to our house, my mother-in-law and the rest of the family greeted us outside.

When we entered the house, I felt like I was in heaven. It was Sangeet night which is when the new bride comes to her husband's house and her in-laws invite everyone to the house to celebrate and sing in happiness. It was full of rejoicing for their son's wedding and their new daughter-in-law. After dinner, the women started singing and then started to persuade me to sing when they heard that I was a good singer. When I started singing, everyone's attention was on me, which I really liked. Raj then surprised me when he started to sing me a love song. It turns out, he had been taking singing lessons without my knowledge to surprise me for this day. By the following evening, all their relatives had left from the house and it became peaceful and quiet. As mentioned earlier, by the third day, the girl has to return to her parents' house to say goodbye to her own relatives and friends who would be waiting for her. So, Danny came to take me home. I stayed there for only one day as Raj was keen to take me back the day after, unlike my real life when Sanjeev did not even turn up. Danny and my parents were sad to see me leave. Although living with my in-laws was a new experience, I was very happy. They were very protective and loving towards me. Raj also made me feel indescribably loved and cared for, which I had never felt in my real life.

As lucky and happy as I was in my pretend life, I was completely the opposite in my real life. I felt unhappy and unwanted, and always followed by bad luck. All my life, I only loved my 5 children and only lived for them. But I hated myself for a long time because I felt that I could not protect them, and it made me feel like I was not a good mother. Sanjeev used to make me feel worse by saying that all I did was deliver so many girls that I did not have time for my son and him anymore. It made me so afraid of paying attention to my daughters. He nagged at me constantly and if he couldn't find anything to nag about, he would then start saying how dusty the house was or find another fault somewhere and blame it on me. He would ask me if I did anything all day except spend time with our daughters.

I never knew what else he wanted. I cooked, cleaned and looked after our children, one of whom had special needs and required more attention. I also took the older ones to school. All Sanjeev did was go to work and when he came home he would not even raise a finger to help. I also had to attend the school parent meetings alone, as well as go to the post office every month to send money for his brothers' education. I was constantly taking the children to the doctors as they would get sick almost all the time. I was very happy to look after my 5 children as well as doing all the housework, but it was impossible to cope with Sanjeev. I walked like a zombie all day with his voice in my head like an electric machine going on and on and I did not know how to turn it off.

After Sanjeev hit 15-month old Anjali, I became even more depressed. I felt so much anger inside me that made me withdraw from my newborn child. I always prayed to God before they were born, asking for them to be healthy, mentally and physically. It did not matter to me if they were going to be a girl or a boy, but all Sanjeev wanted was a boy, even though he never paid any attention to the one he already had; he never found joy in his children.

Even Sanjeev's job was not enough to make him happy. He was an Electrical Design Engineer and received a good salary. When he came home, he would come breathing like a black snake and start criticizing me and the children. We all became very silent as if we were all bitten by the poisonous snake. I have never seen Sanjeev happy for more than a week at a time ever since we were married. So, whenever he was happy, I would pray to God to keep him happy for another week. But, if God listened to unlucky people like me then nobody would be unhappy in this world. I still kept my faith in God even though there was nothing happy about my life, hoping that one day he will change it. We spent five years in Sindri, listening to Sanjeev talking about his generosity towards me and the children; at how he fed us every day and how most men locked their food away from their wives. I have no idea where he heard that from.

One day, while we were still living in Sindri, someone recommended a Specialist to Sanjeev for Asha. The Specialist was located in a different city called Ranchi, so for the very first time Sanjeev took Asha while I looked after the other children. The Specialist prescribed medication for her seizures. He told Sanjeev that because no one had prescribed anything for her seizures for so long, her brain had been weakened considerably. He said its development had slowed down so much that when she turns 20, she would have the mind of a 4-year-old. The doctor asked Sanjeev to bring Asha to him every 6 months to continue with her treatment. Asha turned 57 in 2018 but her mind is still not quite the age of a 4-year-old child. She still does not speak either.

After that visit, we were never able to take Asha back to the doctor again. Sanjeev learned that one of our neighbours was planning to get a visa for England. When he heard that, he found out all the information for himself. He also applied for a visa for himself and the children only. He did not want to take me because he said he wanted to marry an English woman, who could speak to him in English. I never said anything to him. Whatever he said to me, I always kept quiet and absorbed the pain and hurt. That time the children ranged from ages 3 years to 12 years.

The British High Commissioner refused the visa on the grounds they could not allow under-aged children to live abroad without their mother. Sanjeev still had the mindset to not pay anything for me as he felt the dowry money owed to him was given to my sister instead. He tried another tactic to cover my cost by making me write word for word exactly what he wanted me to say to my sister. He made me say that I wanted 2000 rupees for my ticket to England. He also forcefully dictated all these bad things I had to write about her saying she and her husband were mean and they had taken the dowry money that was rightfully his and that if she claims to be the big sister then she should send the 2000 rupees etc. The whole time I thought that I would rip this letter when he wasn't around but as soon as I finished writing, he snatched the letter from me and mailed it. My sister wrote back very upset at me. She also said that she did not have that kind of money and asked why I wanted it as Sanjeev made more money than her husband. I also knew she was never going to help me even if I really needed help because she knew that Sanjeev would never return her money.

CHAPTER 13

Of course, Sanjeev was eager to go to England that he had no choice but to include me. He re-applied for the visa, which we got in early 1969. Our neighbor, Mr. Mann, and his family had left 6 months earlier and had settled down in Nottingham, where his brothers were already living. Sanjeev wrote to him to ask if he could keep an eye on any rental place for us. It was fortunate that a rental place became vacant on the same street as Mr. Mann, 2 days before we left India.

This was the first time I remember that I actually felt some happiness that I was going to leave this life of sorrow behind and was hopeful for a better life in England. As usual though, things did not go smoothly. Sanjeev's father was upset and wanted him to leave our children behind so that he would continue to receive money from him. Sanjeev's father was extremely angry at him when he found out we were taking the children and said that grandparents have more rights than parents. Sanjeev was scared as he knew his father was very forceful and would have definitely taken our children away without any doubt, even from the Airport itself, if he found out when we were leaving. For this reason, we had to quietly leave from Mumbai Airport which was going to take at least a couple of days to get there instead of New Delhi Airport which was only a few hours away. It did not bother other members of Sanjeev's family if he left. My side of the family also did not care whether I stayed or left as they had already detached themselves from me.

It was going to be a long journey to go to Mumbai Airport just to avoid Sanjeev's father, so I made a lot of food and packed it to take with us. We had to catch a bus which took a couple of hours to a town called Dhanbad near Sindri since Sindri did not have any train stations at that time. From Dhanbad we took the train to Calcutta, which took a little less than 6 hours. Then from Calcutta we took the train to Mumbai which took almost one and half days. I was exhausted, and sleep deprived looking after and managing all 5 of our children as we travelled. However, once we were finally on the plane to England on July 17, 1969 I remember feeling a sense of relief. And, it felt absolutely amazing as the plane took off and I knew I was finally leaving India behind.

As the flight started descending when we reached London, England, I remember being quite surprised at seeing the roofs of the houses. They looked like the village roof back home. Once we landed we had to catch a coach from London to Nottingham which took almost 4 hours, then a taxi to where Mr. Mann was living as he did not greet us in Nottingham. We stayed overnight at his house and then the next day we moved immediately into the rented house on the same street. It was a two-storey townhouse. The top floor was occupied by another tenant, so we occupied the main floor. It had two bedrooms and it had a kitchen with a bathtub. The toilet was on the second floor that we had to share with the other tenant.

I was quite disappointed to see the houses and how closed in and small they were. The house we lived in Sindri for the last 5 years was quite large, open with 3 large bedrooms and a big kitchen and bathroom with a separate toilet. The house had a large porch at the front and a big patio and garden at the back of the house. I dreamed that England was going to be like this and much better and was disillusioned when I saw the homes in the area we were living in. But I soon got used to it and started liking Nottingham.

Mrs. Mann was already working in a factory as a seamstress, so Sanjeev asked her if she could find out if they had work for me. She asked her boss, Mr. Jakob the following day. He told her to bring me with her on Monday July 21st to start working. It was only three days after we arrived when I met Mr. Jakob, who then assigned me the job of packing undergarments. I was happy I got the job, but my head spun all day long. I was still jetlagged and fatigued after having to travel for a few days from Sindri to Mumbai and then the 10-hour flight to England with very little to no sleep. The whole time I was looking after the children. Sanjeev himself had gotten sick a couple of days after we arrived so he could not look for a job yet.

At the end of the week, I got my very first pay and was so happy. I was looking forward to giving it to Sanjeev, so I did not even open the envelope. In the undergarment company, 95% of the employees were Indian women and they had a habit of asking each other how much money they made. I was happy to tell them that I wanted to show my husband first. When I came home, Sanjeev was lying in bed. I gave him my pay envelope and said excitedly I got my very first pay today. He threw it away and insulted me in his usual angry way and said, "What money? do you think this is money!?" All my happiness turned into an indescribable humiliation that I still have not forgotten to this day.

It took Sanjeev 6 or 7 weeks to recover from his sickness. He found a job as a TV Repair Technician, but he was not happy in that job. Whenever he applied for a good position, he always got refused on the basis that he was under-qualified. Finally, one company explained the actual reason for their refusal was because they did not accept an Indian degree.

As usual, Sanjeev did not get along with other people so after four months he was fired from his TV Repair Technician job. It was not new for me to hear that as it was his pattern. He was always working 6 weeks here, 4 months there, and the longest time he held a job was in Sindri before we came.

A year later, I found a job at Raleigh. It was a bicycle company which paid more than double the amount I was getting at Jakob's. Thanks to that we were able to purchase our own townhouse on Kimbolton Avenue in 1971 for 2400 pounds. The house had a front-room, living-room and a kitchen on the main floor and two bedrooms and one full bathroom upstairs. The backyard had a small garden and another toilet outside. I later spent a lot of money to convert the outside toilet into a third bedroom with the toilet inside as the children were becoming older. I did not know it at the time, but despite all the changes and payments I had made, Sanjeev only put his name on the house and not mine.

Eventually Sanjeev decided he had to do a MS degree in England in order to get a good job. He applied and was accepted at Nottingham University, near where we lived. Sanjeev was incapable of forming good relationships and communicating with people, but he was very good in education. He finished his MS degree around two years later while I supported the family. After the degree, he applied for engineering jobs but was told that he was over-qualified. Now Sanjeev became depressed, frustrated, and angry. The children and I took all the heat.

I asked Sanjeev why he was so angry with me all the time, to which he replied that "I should know." When I said I did not know and how I could know if he did not tell me, he would then say that it was a wife's duty to know, so if I did not know, then he wasn't going to tell me. I did not know what else I could do for him. I was going to work full time, looking after the children and him, and I never said 'No' to whatever he wanted. I was doing everything possible and whatever he told me to do. I was building bicycle wheels 6 days per week and standing all day. I would leave home at 7:15a.m. and come back home at 4:45p.m. because the factory was only a 15-minute walk from home. I would sometimes come home for lunch just to pay bills and make the mortgage payments during that time. Meanwhile, Sanjeev did nothing, and whatever money he made he would spend it on himself at the pub every day by drinking and spending on others - but nothing for his children or me. Instead, he would take some of my own earnings to continue with his spending.

As soon as I came home in the evenings, he would be standing by the door and waiting for me to make dinner before he would go to the pub. I walked home after standing all day at work; all I wanted was to just sit down and have a cup of tea before starting to make dinner and do the house chores. But I had to force myself to make Sanjeev's dinner first.

Because Sanjeev could not get along with decent, educated people, he surrounded himself with people who could not read or write or even speak good English. They made him feel important and valued. They looked up to him and asked for his help in filling out forms and writing letters. Those people would praise him and tell him how good he was, which made him feel superior. He called them his friends and bought them drinks to make them happier.

When he came home late at night, drunk, he would kick the empty milk bottles outside the front door and would then accuse me of putting the bottles on the wrong side and start calling me bad names. I had been hearing all these insulting words continually said to me, ever since I can remember, which had become increasing vulgar after I was married, so they were not new to me. I think I had become like a stone, so whenever I was insulted or hit, I absorbed the pain. I think God was helping me by giving me the strength to endure it. He would go on and, on all night, repeating it over and over until it was time for me to go to work the following morning. He then spent the whole day sleeping after I left. That was the whole reason I continued to have migraine headaches daily due to lack of sleep. So many times, I wished I had cancer or some untreatable disease, so I could die. I felt it was okay now that my children were safe in England.

My oldest daughter Kajal was 14 years old, and my son Arjun was 13 years and they were both very responsible and very helpful. They helped my two younger daughters, Anjali and Tara, to get ready for school and then would take turns taking Asha to the bus stop to wait for her ride to a special school for the developmentally delayed children. After school, they had to wait for the school bus to pick her back up to bring her home.

CHAPTER 14

After living 5 years in England, Sanjeev saw an ad in the newspaper that Canada needed educated people like doctors, engineers, and professors. The ad said they would pay all the family's fare to fly them to Canada if they qualified. They were holding an information session in Nottingham itself where they invited both husband and wife to attend if they were interested. Sanjeev and I went to the meeting and picked up the forms to apply. We were accepted, and Sanjeev was offered the job. It was an exciting opportunity, so the children and I were happy about moving to a new place. They sent the whole family's flight tickets and arranged an apartment rent free for one month. Sanjeev then put our house for sale through a real estate agent. We had a month to prepare to go to Canada, so it was a very stressful time trying to maintain regular routine of work and school for the children while trying to do all the packing. There were also lots of little things to finalize and close such as bank accounts, giving notices to the schools and work etc.

We had to take a train from Nottingham to London Heathrow Airport for our flight to Canada. It was the month of June 1974 and Sanjeev made me wear two coats.

I was so hot but whenever I tried to take my coat off, he would shout at me and say, "put it back on!". He used to feel ashamed because he was much heavier, and I was underweight at approximately 95lbs. In England some people used to ask him if I was his second wife and if my two older children were from his first wife. He was very envious of me which was why he made me wear the two coats. In the airport everyone was wearing sleeveless tops or dresses and there I was with two coats on. Everyone looked at me as if I was from a different planet.

When we reached Canada, we were greeted by a man from the company who took us to the apartment they were providing. Since I was wearing two coats, he asked if I was cold. He told us that Canada was a lot warmer than England. I could not explain the reason why I was wearing two coats, so I just smiled.

Within 30 days we had to find another apartment. Sanjeev started looking at expensive locations. I told him that we could not afford such expensive places and that he should look at a less expensive apartment, but my opinion did not count. He found an apartment opposite the Ontario Science Centre. It was a 5-bedroom apartment and a very beautiful place all around. But since he could not pay the rent, he told me that I should go out and find a job. He then gave me directions to the unemployment office. It was a new country, new place and new people and it was very difficult for me to go alone but Sanjeev refused to go with me. I had to ask every bus driver which bus to take next. I was surprised how nice the Canadian bus drivers were as opposed to the English bus drivers. When I got to the unemployment office, they were very understanding and helpful, so they sent me to a plastic factory where the manager hired me on the spot. I would start on Monday morning taking Lego pieces off the machine and boxing them.

When I told Sanjeev that I found a job, he asked if I read the contract. I told him that I had signed it, but I could not read all of it as it was too long. He got really mad, shouting and screaming and thumping his hand on the table. The neighbours came by and looked through the windows to see what was happening. The next day, he went with me to see if I actually signed the job contract or something else, but once we got there all he saw was the factory and felt satisfied. I was so hurt by his behavior. I was always forced to go alone everywhere. All he did was to give me orders and directions where I should go. Now he came all the way to the factory to satisfy himself because he could not even trust me to sign a factory job contract.

Before I started my job, we admitted Kajal and Arjun to the local high school and Anjali and Tara to the elementary school. Meanwhile, I found a school for children with special needs, where the government provided free pick-up and drop off taxi for Asha. I then asked a baby sitter who lived in the same building if she could pick Asha up from the taxi in the evenings in exchange for payment as my work was far away. The Lego factory was just outside of Toronto, so I had to leave the house by 6:00a.m. and would only be able to come back home after 6:00p.m. as it would take me at least 2 hours each way from where we lived. I had to take the bus to the subway, then the GO-Train and then from there I had to take another bus and then walk a short distance to the factory. The baby sitter agreed to pick Asha up, but when my other children came home from school they found their sister wandering around the building as she had not been picked up. I had to make arrangements with someone else to keep my daughter until one of my children could pick her up after their school. Despite that, I really liked living in Canada and found the teachers very good at the elementary school. I did not have much contact with the teachers at the high school but both Kajal and Arjun seemed to have adjusted well. I also liked living in Canada better than England as everything seemed so much bigger, brighter and cheerful.

Sanjeev started his new job a few days after we arrived in Canada, but two months later he got into an argument with his boss. Instead of firing him from the company, they transferred him to Guyana in South America at his own expense. They had invested so much money in bringing us all to Canada from England that they felt they would lose out if they let Sanjeev go. They gave him three months to arrange his move to Guyana.

Sanjeev wrote to the real estate agent in England to not sell our house anymore because he wanted to send me and the children back. We did not have enough money to send all of us back together, so he sent my son, Arjun, and my daughter, Anjali, first and two weeks later he sent my oldest daughter, Kajal and youngest daughter, Tara. Finally, two weeks later, Asha, and I returned to England. I put Asha back to the Special Needs School. Since it was a new school year that started in September, both Kajal and Arjun went to college to complete their "A" levels. Now it was Anjali and Tara taking Asha to the bus stop in the mornings and picking her up after school.

Being back in Nottingham, I needed money to look after my children, so the next morning I went to my old factory to ask my manager if I could have my old job back. He said yes, but it didn't turn out to be very good as I did not know that before I returned to England the factory had laid off hundreds of people. So, when other people found out that the manager hired me back, the factory workers got very angry at me. One of the supervisors, Harry, and his wife Joan, were very jealous because so many white people were let go, yet there I was, working there. They started treating me with prejudice and turned people against me. Harry started criticizing me to my manager and making things up, that I was not doing my job, or I was doing something wrong. My manager always used to praise me about how good of a worker I was, but after Harry started smearing my name, my manager and two other supervisors changed and their attitudes towards me became very negative instead.

The people I used to call my friends also started criticizing me, as if I was their enemy. I know most British people were prejudiced at that time but after that, they really made my life unbearable. Although I was working hard and doing more work, I got paid less than the others because Tom, the Supervisor, put most of my work under other women's names. I found out later that they were getting bonus pay that should have been mine and I was getting minimum pay. I put up with them for 11 years more because I needed money to raise my children and pay the mortgage.

Meanwhile, Sanjeev was in Guyana spending all his paychecks on women and drinks. In 1975, the very first year of him working in Guyana, he sent me a total of 150 pounds. It was nothing; not even enough to contribute towards the mortgage. In the second year, he visited us and gave 250 pounds, but every day he went to the pub and asked me for the money. He even asked me to cash Asha's disability allowance and when I said no, he said he was the father, so he should have his signature on it. After that, he did not send any money for the next few years.

When he was in Guyana, some people warned him that he should not get involved with the young women he was with or to go swimming in the same pool as them as they all had Venereal Disease (VD). He did not listen to them and ignored everyone's warning. He ended up with the same disease.

After 3 years in Guyana, he got fired again and returned to Canada to look for work there. That time he visited England again and did not tell me that he had VD. I noticed about a month later I had some spots. I thought they would get better but instead they kept getting worse. I also started feeling very weak but when some people told me that I looked really sick, I went to see my male doctor which I felt embarrassed about. I had no idea what that was and its effect until the doctor sent me to the VD clinic. So, every day for 6 months, I had to go to the clinic after work. When I walked, I felt like I had no strength left in me and all I felt was a dark cloud in front of my eyes.

Sanjeev – being Sanjeev – handled it worse. He wrote me letters blaming me that I gave him VD. Of course, he knew very well that I worked all day and came straight home to look after 5 children. I never even took them to any restaurants or anywhere for vacation and I could never imagine going out without taking them with me. I was still so busy even though Kajal helped me a lot in the kitchen as well as hand washing the clothes, as we did not have a washing machine. I do not know what I would have done without her help.

When Sanjeev came to visit us 6 months later, he admitted that he used to go swimming in the same pool as the prostitutes in Guyana and that was how he got VD. His had gotten really bad and spread into his eyes. He already sought treatment in Canada, but it was of little help. During his visit, I also realized that he was having a hard time finding a job in Canada. Despite his behavior towards me and the children, I suggested that he could look for a job in England. I did not ever imagine that suggestion backfiring on me. He got upset at what I said and then when he returned to Canada, he started sending me letter after letter cursing me. He said that I had put a jinx on him and that was the reason why he could not find a job in Canada. I promised myself that I would never suggest anything to him again.

When Sanjeev finally got a job, he started visiting us every six months for two weeks at a time. Every time he brought a cheque for 3000 pounds and would tell me to sign the back of it so that he could deposit it in his own account. He claimed he did not have any money. He would also make me sign a paper each time stating that he had paid me that amount of money for his own tax purposes. I had to do what he asked me because if I did not then he would make my life hell. And it did not stop there. He started sending abusive letters to me and Kajal calling us prostitutes and other bad names whenever he went back to Canada.

While Sanjeev would visit us during the 2 weeks, it felt like torture. He would elbow me in the middle of the night to get him water. Once he elbowed me so hard, pushing me off the bed onto the floor. Every single night, he would constantly be nudging me as soon as he saw that I was in deep sleep and tell me to either get him water or keep asking me "aren't you going to work?" I would let him know that I had set the alarm, but he did not care and would feel good controlling my sleep. He would then sleep the whole day when I left for work. The children also felt scared sleeping-in as he wanted them all awake in the early hours of the morning. He also looked for any opportunity to keep repeating and arguing about the past how my father did not give him any dowry money and criticizing my family. He would go on about how he has been suffering and how unfairly things have been for him. The two weeks would be really unbearable, and we would all be relieved when he would leave.

As I was not receiving any money from Sanjeev I remembered how my father would tell Veena how he was making his money, so I did the same by buying stocks and shares from the Bank and Telecom where I also made a lot of money.

On one of Sanjeev's visits, he criticized his landlady, saying that she was giving him a hard time. He said that she did not want anyone visiting him and that if he was to call any children to Canada, she was not going to allow them to stay with him. For this reason, he wanted to buy a house but did not have any money to make a deposit. I think he made up the excuse about his landlady so that I had to write him a cheque for 3000 pounds which was all the savings I had at that time. He bought the house and when he came 6 months later, he brought with him legal papers for me to sign. It was to give up my right to have any claim on his house in Canada. I signed all the papers as I did not need or want his house, I only needed peace.

Sanjeev was on and off jobs when my two eldest children, Arjun and Kajal, started university. For that reason, they both qualified for full educational grants. However, when my younger daughters, Anjali and Tara, applied for universities, Sanjeev was already working as an engineer for the CN Rail in the city of Toronto, Canada. He was making $40-45,000 per year which was more than 10 times my income as I was only making 4,000 pounds a year, so they refused any grant. I was constantly struggling to manage the very little money I had. I would sew every piece of clothing the children wore including their winter coats until they went to university. They would sometimes ask if they could buy a piece of clothing from the store, as it would seem very special to them.

I phoned Sanjeev to ask him to send some money for the children's education. I could not believe his answer when he said that he only has one income and he needed it and could not afford to give any money. I told him I also had one income too, which is nothing in comparison to his and was using it to manage all 6 of us. It made him very angry and started telling the children that I was stealing their money. He was referring to the children's child allowance from the 1970's when the British government gave an allowance of 15 shillings to the second child, none to the first child but one pound each week for the third child and every child after that.

When Sanjeev refused to send any money to help Anjali and Tara's education they went to the grant office to explain that I did not receive any financial help from Sanjeev. Tara was a very eloquent speaker and she described and convinced the officer how their father did not support us. The officer was very understanding and therefore he approved the full grant for both of them.

CHAPTER 15

In 1981, Sanjeev called Kajal to Canada after she finished her degree in Biology. She was 23 years old, so Sanjeev was also looking to get her married to a boy from India. Kajal found a job in a laboratory that did testing on cold drinks. Soon after Kajal, he called Arjun to Canada who then got a good managerial job and was also doing a Masters' degree in Math and Computer Science in the evenings at York University.

Sanjeev found a boy named Aditya from India through a matrimonial ad. He arrived two months before the wedding that was scheduled in early February 1982. Sanjeev said he had no money for her wedding, so he told Kajal that she had to pay for the photographer and invitation cards and Arjun had to pay for the food. The temple where the wedding was going to be held was a nominal fee so Sanjeev arranged for the booking of the temple. I had been slowly saving and buying gold jewelry and clothes for my daughter's wedding, so I took that with me because I knew Sanjeev would not be giving anything.

Kajal got married to Aditya but it had not gone smoothly. The weather was really bad, so the photographer did not turn up even though he had already been paid. The food and drinks did not arrive on time either so Sanjeev sent everyone home, but Aditya stood up as they were leaving and apologized as he felt very ashamed at how Sanjeev handled everything. I also felt humiliated and was glad that Aditya's parents were in India, so they did not have to witness it. The guests were mainly Canadian and must have been very shocked at how it all ended and how they were sent home hungry. The food arrived 5 minutes after all the guests had left. Sanjeev was upset and told them to take the food themselves. He did not bother with the fact that it was already paid for and to ask for any compensation. Kajal and Aditya went to a hotel for one or two days and we all went home sadly. Instead of being a joyous occasion it was marked with disgrace and disappointment.

In 1983 both Arjun and I went to India to look for a girl for him, but he did not find a match. So, in 1984, Arjun and Sanjeev went to India to try again and found a girl they liked named Vibha. They got engaged and set the wedding date for the following year in December 1985 to be held in India. Sanjeev did not want me to go to my own son's wedding, but I somehow got the strength from one of my friends, who encouraged me to go. Despite what Sanjeev said, I booked the flight to India to attend the wedding.

In summer of 1986, Sanjeev called Anjali to Canada. She started working in a government job soon after. Later in the same year, someone recommended a boy named Mukesh from India whom she married the following year in September 1987. Even then, Arjun had paid for her marriage and I came from England with jewelry and clothes for her and Mukesh. On the wedding day, Sanjeev arrived from the groom's side instead of being with us to greet them.

Sanjeev had sponsored Kajal, Arjun and Anjali but did not want to sponsor our youngest daughter, Tara, after she finished her degree. He refused blankly because he wanted someone to remain in England so that he would have a place to stay whenever he wanted. I did not want Tara to be alone without her siblings, so I asked my son to try to convince his father, as it was a faster process through him. Arjun begged Sanjeev to just sign the papers and he would do the rest by paying all the expenses involved. He even offered to let Tara stay with him and Vibha, but Sanjeev still refused. After that, my son had no other options except to sponsor his sister who finally came to Canada in 1988.

All my children had left England and I had paid for all their tickets to Canada one by one starting from 1981 to 1988. I was now left alone in England with Asha.

In early 1985 there was a recession in England, so the price of homes had dropped quite a lot. I had applied for a mortgage and when I got approved, I was so happy to have bought a large detached home on Derby Road that I could say was totally mine. The entrance outside of the house had a metal gate with one side of it being the driveway, where you could park two cars in front of the garage itself. On the other side was a small garden where there were rose bushes all around. Once you entered the house it had the family room, living room, a large sun room and a modern kitchen. It was nice to sit in the sun room and look onto the stretch of garden which had different colour of rose bushes lined on one side. The other side was an outside toilet and small decorative bushes. The second floor had 3 bedrooms which were all large, one bathroom and a separate toilet.

I had rented out our house on Kimbolton Avenue to students. Eventually, it became difficult for me to manage both homes, so I asked Sanjeev if I could put the Kimbolton Avenue house for sale which was under his name only. He was happy to do it because he wanted the money and knew the British rule around selling homes were different than the Canadian ones. In Canada the sale of a home is divided equally between the spouses despite whose name is listed as owner(s) of the property whereas in England only the owner gets the money from the sale. I gave the full proceeds of the house to Sanjeev when it got sold in 1986.

I was busy looking after Asha in my new home, however, I started feeling really isolated since Asha was unable to talk or communicate. There was no one I could really talk to as all my children were in Canada. I started water colour painting and writing small books to pass my time. I wanted to join my children in Canada more and more. I started to worry that if I died in England no one would take care of Asha. Sanjeev had totally refused to sponsor us as he wanted a place to stay in England when he retired. He relied on me to still cook, clean and take care of him as well as take all his abuse.

My osteoarthritis had become worse over the 11 years working in Raleigh and I started feeling a lot of pain in my joints. I asked my manager if he could transfer me to another department because of my arthritis and the fact it was getting increasingly difficult for me to carry out my current task. He realized and agreed to transfer me.

When I was transferred to another department at Raleigh, the manager was not very nice and was prejudiced. People took 2-3 days off work because they said they had a cold or flu, but when I requested to take a couple of days off due to the pain and fever, he would not believe me and would refuse even though sick days were unpaid. One day, I hurt my hand so badly that I had to go and see the nurse in the factory. I told her that the arthritis was giving me a lot of pain and problems. I told her that since the factory was laying off so many people I had asked my manager to put my name on the volunteer list to be laid off, but he refused my request and said to me that there was no such thing as arthritis pain. The nurse did not agree with my manager's opinion and said that she would put my name on the list. I thanked her, appreciating that amongst so many bad people there were some nice people too.

The following week, my name came up to be laid off. The women, including the Indian women I worked with were very happy. They were very jealous of me because I was a fast worker and my photo had been printed twice in the factory newspaper. I was happy to leave at the end of October 1986.

Shortly after I was laid off I called the welfare officer who arranged for me to meet him at the Department of Health Services (DHS) office. I had first met him in one of the support meetings that were held once a month for parents with disabled children a while back. I had told him then about my health and work situation. He had been very sympathetic and helpful, so when I met him after I was laid off, he helped to make all the arrangements for support payments for Asha and myself. He was very kind and informed me that I did not have to find another job as the government would support anyone who looked after their sick parents or disabled children. Although I was getting very little money from the DHS allowance, I had peace of mind because I did not have to go to work and could look after Asha much better. To this day, I still have nightmares about working in Raleigh.

CHAPTER 16

My oldest daughter, Kajal who was living in Montreal, Canada with her family, filed for sponsorship for Asha and me in 1989. When I went to the Canadian Immigration officer in England, they told me at the interview that while I could get a visa, Asha could not unless her father applied on her behalf and accepted responsibility to take care of her. My son tried to persuade Sanjeev to sponsor her, but he refused to do anything unless I agreed to sell my own house in England and give all the money to him and live with him in Canada. I refused to do this because I had grown stronger and I also knew he would use all the money for himself, and I would once again be under his thumb. After my refusal Sanjeev became very nasty, and I finally took the decision to file for divorce in 1990. The divorce was settled in early 1991, and I did not ask for a penny in the settlement.

I did not want to come to Canada without Asha, so Kajal had to reapply to sponsor us again in 1990. The process took almost a year. Kajal had hired a lawyer who took our case to the judge. The judge was very surprised by the former decision to refuse me because of Asha, so he immediately approved the visa for both of us. The judge did not even want to hear the details of the lawyer's preparation because he felt that as I owned my own property and had quite a bit of investment savings and was also managing to look after Asha at the same time, there was no reason why we could not come to Canada.

Right after that, I put my house up for sale and a few weeks later I received the visa for Canada. I did not have enough time to wait for the house to sell because I had to enter Canada within 2 months. I had to give authorization to a lawyer to sell the house in my absence. I also had to arrange for a shipping company to ship all my household things to Canada. A week before our flight my son came to England to accompany us on our journey. I landed in Toronto, Ontario, Canada in October 1991 with Asha.

We stayed with my son, daughter in-law, and 4-year-old granddaughter, Neha, in Oakville. In June 1992 my house in England got sold and all the money from it was transferred to my account in Canada. Meanwhile, I was looking for a home and found one close to where my son lived. It was a newly built, 3-bedroom townhouse in Oakville. I paid cash for my house and still had $10,000 left for my rainy days. Asha and I moved into the new house in August 1992. I was very happy to buy my first home in Canada and be closer to all my children. I became busy trying to buy furniture and settle down. I did not even think of Sanjeev and was surprised to find out that he was very angry at my son when he found out I had bought a home in Canada. He demanded why Arjun had called me here. Arjun was the only one who was maintaining a connection with Sanjeev, so he would get the brunt of his anger even though Kajal was the one who had sponsored me.

I joined a Child Care Agency to look after children at home because I could not go out to look for a job as I was caring for Asha. I arranged for her to go to a Special Needs Centre between 9:00a.m. to 3:00p.m. from Monday to Friday while I babysat. I took Asha to a specialist who tested and officially diagnosed her as being developmentally delayed with severe autism and an inability to talk. She was also diagnosed with Obsessive Compulsive Disorder (OCD) which manifests itself by the compulsion to tidy everything up all the time. If Asha was not sleepy at night she would wander around the house looking for things to tidy, such as the pots in the kitchen or the unwashed laundry.

I was 50 years old with arthritis and other health issues; it was very tiring to babysit 4 or 5 really young children for 11 hours a day from 7:00a.m. to 6:00p.m., but I somehow managed. Both my daughter and I were taking a lot of medicine and it was costing me a lot of money without any health insurance coverage. So, once again my son had to go to his father. He asked him if he could cover Asha in his company's drug plan, since she was his dependent. Sanjeev refused and said that if I could not manage, I should go back to England, even though including Asha in his insurance would have cost him next to nothing. Because of this my son started giving me $500 a month in 1995 for almost a year until the time Anjali separated from her husband and moved in with me in November 1996. She had two young daughters, Kiran and Priya and was pregnant with her third child. Anjali did not want me to babysit anymore as it would be too much for me, with her children to look after. She said she would help manage the expenses with me instead.

However, Asha's and my medical expenses were still too costly, and I did not want to put too much pressure on Anjali because she was now a single parent herself. Since my son was the only one talking to Sanjeev, he tried to persuade his father to start paying child support for a disabled dependent as Asha really needed expensive medicine. As usual, Sanjeev refused.

I hired a lawyer to help me get dependent child support from Sanjeev, but, the lawyer informed me that I had to go through the court system and become Asha's legal guardian first as she was 35 years old and incapable of making decisions for herself. Once I became her legal guardian I filed the court papers with the help of my children and the court lawyer in January 1997 for child support. The Judge granted $500.00 a month from Sanjeev effective February 1997. It included $300 as child support and $200 for me even though I had not requested it. I think the judge felt that I should have some compensation for the extensive responsibility that I had for looking after Asha all by myself. I did appreciate it very much but eventually stopped the $200 payment for myself when it was no longer necessary.

Meanwhile Sanjeev was getting very angry at Arjun why he helped me to get the child support through the court. He started phoning Arjun, arguing and verbally abusing him, so Arjun stopped talking with him. However, Sanjeev would not stop there and from time to time wrote long letters to Arjun cursing him and his daughter. When he realized he wasn't getting anywhere with that approach, he found out my telephone number from the court papers and started calling me. He would ask if he could live with me by saying that couples in this country stay friendly. I was now wiser and understood his soft approach, which I knew did not mean anything except to serve his own purpose. I said no, and he immediately put the phone down on me.

After that, Sanjeev bribed his youngest sister, Tanuja, who was in India, that he would sponsor her son to come to Canada if she helped him get me back to him. He asked Tanuja to persuade me to live with him again. So, Tanuja started writing to me and when she did not receive any replies, she started phoning me almost every day in the middle of the night. She did not care what time it was, all she wanted was to talk to me about Sanjeev. She said that he needed me to look after him because he was not feeling well. But my divorce from Sanjeev after 35 years of abuse had made me strong. I stopped answering the phone altogether. After that Sanjeev became friendly with Arjun again and started working on him. He asked Arjun to tell me to stop the court-required payments for Asha because he would pay me more money per month. Of course, I now understood and knew that he would not pay. He was already complaining about paying $500 through the court system so he could not possibly be willing to pay more.

In January 2000 I had my first stroke which left my left side weak. I could not walk or even lift a glass of water. It took 6 months of physiotherapy for me to start walking normally again, although my numbness lasted 10 more years and I still have weakness in my left leg to this day. Then four years later, in May, I had my second stroke. It made my left leg even weaker and took around 2 months of physiotherapy to re-strengthen. Around a year later, I had a mini stroke where I stayed in the hospital for the day and the doctor prescribed blood thinners. The doctors said that if I had another stroke there was a possibility it would leave me paralyzed or unable to speak. I was beside myself thinking what would happen to Asha if I wasn't able to look after her myself. This has always been a constant fear for me as I do not want to leave her behind. I also do not want my children to feel pressured to look after her either as they have their own families to look after.

My daughter Anjali and my three grandchildren, Kiran, Priya and Rohan who was born in 1997, lived with me and Asha for 6 years in the 3-bedroom town house. But as they grew older, they needed their own space. We decided to buy a new home in 2001 that was going to be built the following year which was only a 5-minute drive from the townhouse. The builder's floor plan was for a 4-bedroom home with the option of making the open space into a 5-bedroom. We requested the builder if it was possible to convert the upstairs laundry room into a 6-bedroom as we needed it for all of us. We were happy they were able to accommodate our request, even though we had to pay for all the additional changes, but we felt fortunate they were able to do it. In August 2002, the house was completed and we all moved into our new home. My grandchildren were all very happy that they got their own bedrooms, but they still miss the townhouse to this day as they remember the closeness we shared in the small house.

In March 2003, when the children were at there father's house, Anjali and I went to buy a puppy for them. When they returned, the were overjoyed to see the puppy as they always wanted to have a dog, in particular Kiran. He was a Bichon poo, we named Lucky.

CHAPTER 17

I had been inviting my sister and brother to Canada for quite a while despite how they had been towards me. Veena did finally come in spring 2003 to visit me but Vijay did not want to come. I was happy to see my sister and we took her to all the usual tourist sites around us, such as the CN Tower, Rogers Centre, Niagara Falls, Ottawa Tulip Festival, Strawberry picking etc. Instead of being happy, Veena was jealous and started putting me down. When she saw me helping my granddaughter's English homework she ridiculed me and said I was so stupid before so how I could possibly become clever. Also, when Veena found out the framed water colour paintings Anjali had hung around our home were painted by me, she sarcastically asked how I could be capable of painting them.

She continued to also state why I divorced Sanjeev as I should be thankful to him as he had brought me here otherwise I would still be rotting in India. She also unrelentingly blamed me for her 1 ½ year old son's death as she claimed that she was making ladoo for me while I was in the hospital when Arjun was born. She said it was for this reason she could not watch over her son when he ate some soap. He died a few months after eating it that the doctors had indicated was the reason for his death. However, her insinuation was far from the truth as she had never cooked for me and had not even come to see me when my son was born.

She stayed with me for 3 months and then went back to India. A few years later she started writing to me and asked that I go to India to see her before she died as her health had started deteriorating. I had gone to India a few times before and always made sure I visited my sister and brother. But, whenever I went to India to see her she would still remind me even though she was ill, that her son had died when my son was born. I feel very hurt to not have had the courage to speak up for myself, but for some reason, I seemed to be trapped in the cycle of not being able to say anything whenever I got hurt. However, I still went to see my sister in 2013 because of her health. I did feel a little sadness but did not shed any tears when she passed away the following year in August 2014. However, I don't remember having any tears either when my brother had died in 2011 nor for my father when he had died in 1975 of heart attacks. It was strange that my father-in-law also passed away 6 months after my father as they always hated each other in this world, so I often wonder whether they still hate each other where they are now. Also, in the late 1990's my mother-in-law had died when the brick walls of her house fell on top of her while she was sleeping. It was ironic how she died as I remember once when Sanjeev left me in the village to live with her, she was very angry with me and had started beating her chest and screaming at me that if I wanted to live there, I should pay her 100 rupees for each brick. It was not my choice to live there in the first place, but I was forced to. She had kept going on and on until I could not take it any longer, and in my frustration, I spoke back saying she should take all the bricks with her when she dies and that is exactly how she had died.

My granddaughter, Kiran, was excited to decorate her own bedroom. She selected the colour of her drapes, bedding and had shopped for ornaments and had put stars up on the wall and ceiling that would glow in the dark. She had chosen her study desk and lamp and put photos of the family in her room. Unfortunately, she did not get a chance to enjoy it long enough.

She got hit on her head extremely hard two days in a row by a soccer ball in the school playground. I don't know if it was intentional or not. But on the second time, Kiran was complaining even more than the first time that her head hurt a lot, and she was feeling weak. She did not feel she could go to school the next day. This was unusual for her. However, it shocked us when Anjali suddenly felt the bed shaking in the middle of the night and witnessed Kiran having a seizure. It was the beginning of a lengthy period of going to Sick Children's Hospital in Toronto to find out why. It was a very unique condition the doctors did not know of. She would have mini seizures only when she was shocked, for example when a balloon suddenly popped or when there was a sudden sound, or the car had to do an emergency stop. She became a subject of the doctors' investigation and is reported in their medical journal.

Kiran had just celebrated her 14th birthday in February 2005 and was scheduled for brain surgery the following month on March 21st at Sick Children's Hospital in Toronto to help with the seizure. The surgeon initially came out and told her parents, Anjali and Mukesh, that everything was fine. He even said they could see her in the recovery room soon. But between then and midnight, something went horribly wrong. She never woke up from her surgery. The doctors informed Anjali and Mukesh they did not know why there was sudden brain swelling and therefore had to put her on life support. We did not know at that time she had technically died. Arjun and Vibha picked me, Priya and Rohan and rushed to the hospital. Tara was already there as she was living in Toronto and Mukesh's family also came to the hospital.

The doctors officially disconnected the life support from Kiran on March 22, 2005. Neha was on her school trip in Mexico and her parents did not have the heart to tell her until she returned. Kajal's family were all living in Texas, US and were also unable to come as everything was so sudden. However, Kajal did make it to the funeral that was held a couple of days after.

Kiran was only 4 years old when she had first started living with me. We did so many things together along with Priya and Rohan over the 10 years before she died. She left so many memories that not a day goes by that I don't remember her. Now I am 71 years old, in 2013, and I am wishing that when I leave this world the first person I see is my granddaughter.

In the same tragic year that Kiran passed away, I found out Tara was diagnosed with breast cancer. It was heartbreaking to see Tara, my youngest daughter, go through chemotherapy, radiation and mastectomy. It was also very hard to hear her say that she felt so unlucky, just like I had felt throughout my life. Nothing seemed to go right for her, from friends at school, relationships, work, and health. And this new challenge was no different. She had to wait for one year after her mastectomy to have breast reconstruction, however, one female doctor suggested that she could have it done after 6 months only. Tara wanted to get it done as soon as possible so she decided to go to her. But it went horribly wrong. She started losing her breast flesh. She had to be connected to a machine that would remove the loose flesh and help build new one. She had to walk, sleep, eat, and breathe with it 24 hours a day for approximately 5-6 months. She was totally devastated and emotionally broken down. She then had to wait over two years before they could even start the process to do breast reconstruction by beginning to build and expand her skin. It was a very long and difficult time she had to go through. It wasn't until 2009 that she finally had her reconstruction surgery done.

CHAPTER 18

till, I continue to go to my pretend life as my real life is filled with so much sadness. My pretend life helps me to escape into a happier state of mind where I can get some form of peace. Here I was loved not only by my husband, but also by all his family and friends. That kind of love is very hard to forget.

Raj's brother, Harry, did not finish his degree but did get married to the girl he was dating named Nina. Now Raj and I have been married two years and I was expecting our first baby. Both sides of our families were looking forward to seeing our new baby as all the other children had grown up. But we all know even the happiest people - rich, poor or royal - all have their ups and downs so there was happiness and sadness, even in my pretend life. I lost my first pregnancy because of Nina's jealousy. In her mind, she thought that our in-laws liked me better. She also wanted my husband for herself. To get me out of the way, she pretended to be my friend and always gave me food and drinks. Little did I know that she had started mixing poison in it. I got sicker and sicker by the day, but neither Raj nor my doctor could figure out why. The poison she gave me was untraceable which caused me to miscarry when I was only 3 months pregnant.

Ramu Kaka, my childhood housekeeper, had moved with me after I got married. I was happy he was around as he always took really good care of me. One day he saw Nina mix something in my tea and then hide the vial in her bra. Ramu Kaka immediately told my father-in-law, who took the tea from my hand and then called Raj to have it tested. Raj called the police who searched Nina's room where they found the poison and a diary where she had been writing. In it, Nina had written all her plans. First, she was going to kill me and get close to Raj by comforting him; secondly, she was going to kill her own husband, Harry, so that Raj would get close to her by comforting her; and the third step was to kill our father-in-law. She had written that killing our mother-in-law would be very easy, as she would be half dead after losing her son and husband. Nina was immediately reported to the police and tried by a judge. Because of her plans to kill four people in the family, she was sentenced to life imprisonment.

For me the damage was already done as I had lost my baby. I also stayed very sick for a long time afterwards. But with my family's love and support, I got better one day at a time. After a year, I got pregnant again so both Raj and I were excited. Both our families were too and did not want me to do anything except rest and enjoy myself. Nine months later I gave birth to a healthy baby boy, we named Neel. Everybody was happy, especially my father-in-law. He threw a very big party for our family, friends and neighbours for the birth of his grandson.

All of the happy events in my head made me think about my real children, all five of them. Nobody ever cared or asked me to rest while I was pregnant. I went back to doing so much housework right after they were born, and nobody was ever happy or excited except for me. Instead, everyone, including my mother-in-law, sisters-in-law, and even Sanjeev, shamed me, and taunted me about having all these girls. However, even when I had a son, they still did not show any happiness around him, let alone throw him parties. All those memories still hurt, which is why I still could not give them my full attention, especially my daughters. It took me all these years to realize I never had to listen to him when it came to showing affection to my children. The only thing that had stopped me from killing myself was the anger I felt when my own mother died and left me when I was only two years old. I did not want to do the same thing to my children. I would rather die with them, then leave them behind.

Since I divorced Sanjeev in 1991, I have been in peace. Now and again, he still disturbs Arjun and Kajal by saying insulting things about me which they don't want to hear. When Sanjeev phones Kajal, she gets very emotional because it reminds her of how badly he had treated her. Also, the fact that he did not take any interest in her or his own grandchildren or even ask how they were, never mind knowing their names. He had even written in his divorce papers that he did not have any children and they were not his. Yet, he would still harass them. It still hurts me and makes me angry about everything Sanjeev did to us, or didn't do, for that matter.

In 2013, Asha turned 52 and remained very active as no medication seemed to have controlled her OCD tidying behavior. She is unable to speak or communicate and just makes noises but is very gentle and does not harm or hurt anyone. If we try to stop her from doing something wrong, she would scream very loudly, and it would give people the wrong impression that we are hurting her. It has been sad to see her life passing in the silence of her own mind. Her OCD has also made it difficult at times to call people or friends over to the house because of her behavior. She would take their drinks or plates away from their hands or from the table before they even finished. Her OCD caused her anxiety, so as she grew older she had become a little more impatient about waiting for them to finish in order to put everything away. It was even hard to use clean dishes as one minute she would be tidying the garbage bins and then the next touching the clean dishes and utensils with the same hands.

I started looking for a place for Asha before my health could get worse as I did not want to restrict and burden my children with the responsibility I shouldered my whole life. Unfortunately, the residential places I applied for refused to admit Asha based on her OCD and the loud noises she makes. I am not scared of dying, but I am scared of leaving Asha behind.

Despite the challenges with Asha's care, I am very happy with all my children and how they look out for each other. My youngest daughter, Tara, who lives in Toronto, gives me a break from time to time by looking after Asha while I go to Texas to visit Kajal. My second youngest daughter, Anjali, would often take time off work to take us to doctors and specialist appointments. She also looks after Asha when I visit my sister in India or visit Kajal. Sometimes my son, Arjun and daughter in-law, Vibha, also help to take us for appointments.

CHAPTER 19

So many times, I wanted to stay in my real life, but in my mind, I felt like I was imprisoned for life, so I felt like the only escape for me was to go into my pretend life.

In this pretend life my son, Neel, was already born. I stayed home to take care of him, although his grandparents were very happy to look after him too. I was a very excited new mother and I couldn't stay away from him, so I opened a law practice from home.

Around this time, Raj told me that he saw someone working at the hospital who looked like my best friend, Maya. So many years had passed since Maya and I got married that we lost contact with each other. When we were both in the same university, Maya fell in love with a boy who wasn't very nice. I tried to warn her that she would not be happy with him, but she was so much in love with him that she did not want to take my advice. As soon as she finished her degree in nursing, she married him. When Raj told me the woman he saw looked in bad shape, I got a bad feeling. I wanted to find out if it really was Maya, so the next day I went to the hospital to find out.

I recognized her immediately when I saw her, but she did not recognize me. Or maybe she only pretended not to because she felt ashamed. The clothes under her nursing uniform were looking tattered and dirty. When she finally recognized me, I gave her a big hug and apologized that I did not keep in touch. I asked how she had been and as she started telling me everything, she could not hold back her tears and started crying.

She told me her father had passed away soon after she married, while her brother, Jagdesh, and his wife, Urmila, and two children continued living with their mother. She said soon after getting married she immediately started having problems with her husband. Apparently, he started drinking and going to clubs with other girls. She said her in-laws did not like her and also blamed her for their son's behavior.

It had gone so bad between Maya and her husband, so they ended up divorcing and she had to move back to her mother's house. Maya said her mother was very worried about her being divorced so young and wanted to help Maya remarry. However, soon after Maya moved back home, her mother died from a heart attack. It left Maya feeling alone even though she was now living with her brother and sister-in-law. She said it was okay for a while but eventually her brother started controlling her and taking her paycheck. He stopped her from going out and talking to any men, even to say hello. He said she was a divorced woman, so he was worried what people would say. Soon her brother and sister-in-law also started taking advantage of her presence. She would come home, tired from work, and be expected to cook, do household chores, and look after their two young children while they went out almost every evening. Maya said she even had to ask her brother for new clothes. But even if he did buy her new clothes, his wife would take them and give Maya her old ones instead. She would remind Maya that she should not be wearing any new clothes, being a divorced woman, as she could give the wrong impression to men.

I asked Maya to come and live with me, but she was afraid of her brother. So, I promised her that I would come soon and see her again. That night, I could not sleep without thinking about Maya and why I let her go back to suffer more. I remembered that when I first met her, I had been in worse condition, as my brother and I had been on the street and were about to drown ourselves before our new adoptive parents spotted us. I understood what she was going through and wanted to help her. She had been my adoptive parents' neighbour's daughter and I had been so happy to see another girl that we immediately became very good friends - almost like sisters. All night I was thinking about how I could help her.

The next day, Danny and I spoke with Maya and convinced her that she was able to stand on her own two feet. We told her that we knew it would be difficult at first but convinced her that, in the end, she would be much happier than being controlled by her brother and sister-in-law.

Raj and I helped Maya move out of her brother's house against his disapproval and anger into our guest room. Next day, I went shopping with Maya to buy her new dresses and sari's and she opened a bank account to keep her money in. It felt like old times when we used to do everything together and we were both very happy.

It was nice having Maya around and seeing her feeling free living with me. Her brother tried to convince her to return home every so often, but his main intention was to get her monthly paycheck and have her look after his children. By this point, Maya had grown confident and strong living away from him and told him that she had her own life to live. He blamed me, saying that I was responsible for teaching Maya to stay away from him. He even accused me of taking advantage of her and her money. But I did not care what he thought as I knew I was only helping my best friend. During this time, I also had my second son, Sunil.

Another two years had passed when Raj told me his friend, Dr. Verma was getting a divorce. I wasn't surprised since his wife was ill-mannered and rude to everyone. I always liked Dr. Verma because he was very nice and always very polite. I introduced Maya to Dr. Verma and their relationship grew stronger and they decided to marry. Maya phoned Jagdesh to tell him the good news in the hopes of making amends. Instead, he got angry at Maya and told her that he had nothing to do with her anymore and that she was dead to him. Maya was sad that her brother did not attend her wedding but appreciated us being there for her instead. She looked absolutely beautiful when she got married.

One night in my pretend life we had a dinner party for our friends. I was about to have my third child, whom I hoped was a girl, and we thought it was a great opportunity to celebrate before I would get busy with my new born and both my sons who were now 6 and 3 years old. After dinner, while we were just sitting and talking, I started feeling uncomfortable. My brother-in-law, Pradeep, who is also a very good doctor, noticed and told Raj. He suggested that Raj should take me to the hospital. Everyone laughed and said they would come with us.

My daughter Jain was born a week early. It became a very memorable day for me as all our doctor friends and spouses were at the hospital with me. I was taken into a private room with the baby when my parents and in-laws arrived. They wanted to stay with me and their granddaughter all night, but the doctor said they would have to leave as the baby and I needed full rest. Everybody left except Raj who stayed with us the whole time. Every time I woke up I saw Raj looking at the baby and it seemed like he loved his daughter so much that he could not take his eyes away from her. He was a proud father. I also felt very happy and thought how beautiful and special she looked.

Early next morning my parents, in-laws, friends, and family visited us again. On the third day I came home from the hospital. As much as I was loved and surrounded by family and friends in my pretend life, I could not stop thinking about my real life and how totally different and sad the same circumstances were. But if I had everything I wanted in my real life I would not have created this pretend life… but it is what it is and there was no point thinking about it as it was just my bad luck and my pretend life was helping me to cope with my real life.

Now my eldest son, Neel, was going to school and the other two children were being looked after by their grandparents. Raj and I had also made a lot of money with our jobs as a doctor and a lawyer. I was looking for a new challenge and a new way to make money, so I had an idea to open a boutique. The store would have everything from make up to designer clothes, handbags and shoes. Raj and my in-laws liked my idea, so I immediately started looking for a good location and designers I could feature in the shop. I named the boutique store after our daughter, Jain.

Soon it was set up and after a few years our hard work was paying off as Jain Boutique started gaining recognition, it also started making a lot of money. I then had the idea to use this money and expand our business to a new expensive high-end restaurant. This time I chose to name it after our second son, Sunil. We hired a manager and found a really good chef as well as professional staff to ensure the restaurant ran well. Soon after, the restaurant also started succeeding. After that I wanted to do two more things: first was to open a hospital under Neel's name and second was to open a new temple under my father-in-law's name as he had given me so much love and respect, which I wanted to honour. The rest of my pretend life was running very well but from time to time my mind would go back to my brother, Ravi. I would think about his life whether he was happy or sad, dead or alive and where he would be living. Sometimes I would think the only way I could ever find him, was if he had become a criminal.

Since my papa was a police chief he would sometimes call on me to help with his cases as I had the gift of seeing through people. This helped when the police found it difficult to determine if the criminals were really guilty or not. I would often wish one of the criminals would be Ravi and always get disappointed when it was not.

The biggest gang in Delhi would often come into the city from their hide out in the mountains and threaten and steal from the banks and rich people. They were creating a lot of stress in the police force for their capture. One day my papa and his staff caught one of the members, so he called me to help question him. When I saw him in jail, he immediately asked me to help him find a lawyer. I felt a strange connection with him the moment I saw him, so I said I would be able to represent him myself.

The very first thing he whispered to me was to ask for some paper and a pen. He wrote that he meant to get caught and informed me that a lot of high-profile police officers were mixed with the robbery gang to help them escape or inform them that police were on their way. He also wrote that his jail was bugged and that the police had put a man in the opposite jail to keep a watch on him so that he would not reveal anything. He continued to write that he had seen the same man talking to the leader of his robbery gang. He also said he would tell me everything if I took him somewhere safe, but if he stayed in jail he was scared that he would be taken back to his gang or killled. I took the written paper from him and hid it in my handbag and went to see my papa in his office.

My papa was speaking with another officer and asked me if I found out anything more about the robber and his gang. I said no. I asked my papa if I could take him out to conduct my own cross-examination, but the officer suddenly got very angry and said that he was a dangerous man and that he should not be allowed to leave prison. His reaction gave me the answer to my suspicions: he was also involved with the robbery gang.

Later, I gave the written paper to my papa and told him that the gang member was telling the truth. My papa said he also suspected that they must be getting help from someone inside the police department as every time they came close to getting the robbers, they would get away somehow.

The next day I went to see the man in the jail as his lawyer. I asked him to answer all the questions that I had prepared for him including his name, how he had joined the robbery gang and why he wanted himself to get caught. He wrote all the answers plus more information about his parents, siblings and his childhood. He also showed me a newspaper photo of himself that he had on him. Suddenly I knew why I felt connected to him. I had seen this newspaper photo before because my brother Danny had this photo too. He wrote that his aunt had sold him to the robbery gang, who gave him a different name and cut his forehead with a knife so that no one would recognize him. He said there was a butler in the gang's house who treated him kindly. It was this man who gave him the newspaper photo and told him to remember his real name, Ravi. It turns out that the gang leader taught him how to rob but he also gave him a good education. As I learned more about him, I realized he was my long-lost brother who had been sold when he was 5. He was now a tall young man with a beard and his hair was shoulder length and even though his hair looked overgrown you could see his good features.

I could not wait to tell Danny. That day felt so long for me, waiting for him to come home. When I finally got to show Danny, Ravi's written paper and photo, he immediately compared the newspaper photo he had. We screamed together, fully realizing we had finally found our lost brother.

That same night we went to see our parents and told them everything. My papa said we should think of a plan quickly before the robbers take him out themselves. I then came up with the idea that my papa could celebrate my upcoming birthday at the police station hall. We would bring a huge birthday cake to give to all the officers and another cake mixed with lots of sleeping tablets for the guards and prisoners around my brother's jail. Everyone liked my idea because they could not think of anything else. I knew it was deceitful, but we were saving my innocent brother, so it was worth it. I told Ravi about our plan and to be prepared to escape quickly.

There was lots of music, dancing and celebration during my birthday party at the police hall. While the rest were feasting, Danny arranged for the other cake with the sleeping tablets to be delivered to the guards and prisoners. Danny took the keys from the guard when they had all fallen asleep and opened the jail to let Ravi out. He brought Ravi to my house. Nobody suspected anything and didn't realize that Ravi was not in jail anymore.

The festivities ended after midnight and we all went home. I found Ravi waiting for us when we arrived. We had a long talk and then I told him who we really were; that I was his sister and Danny his brother. I often used to think that something was missing from my life. Now it was complete and there was nothing more that I wanted.

Danny, Ravi and I talked all of the following day, reminiscing about the past and dreaming about what we would do in the future. My papa said he always wanted two sons and now his family was complete. We were all happy, laughing and joking.

Soon after we arranged Ravi's and my tickets to America to get plastic surgery to remove the scar on his forehead. We all knew that while he had it, none of us would be safe as both the police and gang were looking frantically for him and handing out photos. We also knew that if we had done the surgery in India, anyone could bribe the plastic surgeon and find out everything about Ravi.

The police continued searching for Ravi while we were in America. As my papa was the head of the police department, he had to pretend he was furious about the prisoner getting out of the jail. He also told them that his brother had just died so he was going to call his brother's son to live with him as he never got along with his step mother. So, when Ravi and I came home, no one was suspicious.

For his part, Ravi started to make peace with his new life. I could still feel how much Ravi had suffered since he was taken away from us, but we both decided that the past is the past and we were now here for each other. We knew we were fortunate to have a happy ending as so many other people do not even get that chance. Ravi was also appreciative that the butler had told him about his family and felt grateful to him.

Soon Ravi wanted to get a job, get married and settle down so we started to look for a suitable girl for him. I remembered when I had my daughter, there was a nurse in the hospital called Shanti who was beautiful, down to earth, and very quiet. The other nurses put her down because she was from a poor family and she could not dress like the other nurses. Ravi was also very down to earth himself so I knew he would like Shanti. I asked her to come for lunch and introduced her to Ravi. They liked each other so they started to go out together.

I asked Ravi to work in our restaurant, but he was determined to be my driver and bodyguard because, as a successful lawyer, I also had enemies. I had never lost a case, but some criminals did not like that, so Ravi was worried about me and my family. He also persuaded me that he really wanted to protect me because he wasn't there for me before. I said okay, as I knew I could not trust anyone else better than my own brother.

My children were growing very fast and doing very well at school. I did open a hospital under Neel's name, which was running well, and my law practice was doing great. I suggested to Raj that since we had enough money we should build a temple under my father-in-law's name. I always took my in-laws permission before I did anything as their blessing was very important to me, although I knew they would never say no to anything I asked.

As Ravi was living with our parents and getting closer to Shanti we started to make plans for their marriage. After Ravi got married, we all helped him buy a house close to us which made me feel happy. I now had both my brothers living near me. The robbers were still looking for Ravi and handing out photos and asking around if anyone had seen him, but I wasn't worried because Ravi did not look the same anymore.

CHAPTER 20

In my pretend life, my sons, Neel and Sunil, were now in university studying medicine and business respectively. Both have also found their life partners. Soon my daughter Jain will be starting university too and wanted to follow the same steps as I did by studying law. She is beautiful, talented, with a good head on her shoulders and a kind nature that makes everyone love her. She also has talent for music and dance. She started liking Raj's best friend's son, Pratik, who was already studying medicine. I always liked Pratik and had wished in my heart that one day he should be my son-in-law, so it was nice to see my wish was coming true. Raj and I had never forced our children about what to do because they were already very wise and clever, and we were very happy and proud at how well they were doing.

After Neel finished his medical degree and specialized as a surgeon, he started working in his own hospital. My mother-in-law really wanted Neel to get married now. She was getting old and sick and wanted to see at least one grandson's marriage. So, we got busy preparing Neel's wedding. It was the first marriage in our family so everyone was happy and excited. Neel's grandparents were so happy that they spent a lot of money throwing the biggest party in the neighbourhood. After that, my mother-in-law started hoping she would live long enough to see her great grandchild. Luckily, she did, as Neel had a baby boy shortly before she passed away. After she was gone, I made sure that Raj and the children never let their grandfather feel lonely. I loved my father-in-law as he had always treated me like his own daughter.

A year later, Sunil finished his business degree, so we gave him the restaurant to run. We also started preparing for his wedding during this time. My father-in-law was as excited as he was during Neel's wedding and wanted to throw another big party, but this time my mother-in-law was not around to be by his side, so we all helped him as much as we could. We made sure that he would not feel my mother-in-law's absence in Sunil's marriage.

Now both Neel and Sunil had gotten married, so Raj and I decided that we should buy each of them a house similar to ours. We also thought that eventually, Jain could have our house since she always liked it.

As my children began their adult lives, my parents progressed into old age. My papa became very sick, so I was worried about losing them. I would visit them 2-3 days a week, but it did not help me from worrying. I am still glad that I can share my worries with both of my brothers, which really helped.

Now Jain had almost finished her degree and she was getting serious with Pratik, so his parents suggested they should get engaged while Pratik finished his medical degree.

He was specializing in neurology which would take another two years before they could get married.

Neel was expecting his second child, a baby girl, while Sunil's wife was expecting their first child. I was a happy and excited grandmother. But all that happiness died when I heard the news that my papa had been rushed to the hospital. Immediately my brothers and I went over to see him. We were all worried. My mother sat at my papa's bed side in tears and we tried to comfort her as much as we could. This time he survived, but the doctors told us that next time he was not going to be so lucky. We were happy that at least we had our papa back, especially my mother.

After Jain finished her law degree, we celebrated her engagement with Pratik. Pratik's parents, Dr. Rajinder and Nirmala, were very close friends and now that our children were engaged, we were happy to become very close relatives. My father-in-law's health was declining at this point, so I prayed that he and my parents would live much longer so they could see their only granddaughter wed. When Pratik finished his degree and started working in our hospital, we finally started preparing Jain's wedding.

I asked Jain if she wanted anything special for her wedding, like my papa had asked me. All Jain wanted was an unforgettable reception, so Raj and I asked our families opinion. Her grandparents had different opinions and it was hard to please everyone. In the end Raj and I decided that we would arrange the venue for the ceremony and reception with my brothers' and brother-in-law's help. We rented a cricket field and hired the best decorator possible. It looked so beautiful with lights and decorations that were astounding. The room was also filled with a multitude of colourful flowers and chandeliers. Jain really liked how the whole reception looked, especially when she heard her friends say how they had never seen such a beautiful wedding reception before.

During the big day, both Jain and Pratik looked very beautiful together. There were so many people who joined the celebrations as well, even some who were uninvited. But everyone was welcome to eat, as we had an abundance. We had no fear either, because my papa had so many police around the area for security. My daughters' wedding turned out to be the most wonderful day and I was happy that Jain was also in a loving family, like I was in.

After Jain's marriage, Raj did not want me to work as a lawyer anymore and asked if I could work with him at the hospital. I agreed because I wanted to work with my husband and it was also safer than working at the law firm with criminals. Also, it would be easier for Ravi as he would no longer need to worry about me and my safety.

One day my father-in-law got very sick that he had to go to the hospital. I could wish as much as I wanted but I knew I could not stop old age. My father-in-law died within 24 hours and it was a great loss filled with sadness that he would no longer be around. My wish was that I should die before my husband and brothers.

As we were all getting old, it made me want to finish all my unfinished business, so I suggested to Raj that while we were healthy, we should divide our assets to our children. Raj agreed that it was a good idea, so we officially gave the hospital to Neel, the restaurant to Sunil and the Boutique to Jain. Also, we had given them one house each.

Soon after, my papa got sicker and passed away peacefully in his sleep. My mother took it hard. I feared she would not live much longer because she stopped wanting to live without him. My brothers and I tried to be around her often, but she still felt lonely without my papa. I did not blame her as he was the nicest papa and husband anyone could have, and I missed him also. That was why I advised my children that when I leave this world, they should take care of their father and not to let him feel alone.

A year after my papa died, my mother passed away also. It was a great loss. I felt as if I lost my real parents. I felt like I was two years old again because my pretend parents were very real to me, more real than my real life and I would never forget that.

Now I am concentrating on the rest of my family, my husband, children, and grandchildren. I just heard good news that Jain had a baby boy and I could not be any happier. I am now a grandmother for all my children. Raj and I both retired and spend most of our time with our grandchildren.

CHAPTER 21

So many times, I forced myself not to think about my pretend life and that I should just stay in my real life. But my mind goes back to my pretend life as fast as the blink of an eye. Maybe it's because of my worries with Asha. Or maybe in my real life I have such bitter memories because of Sanjeev. Between his insults, calling me words I cannot even write, and his threats toward me and the children. I still have a lot of hurt and pain. Every night I used to get humiliated and shamed by him insulting me with the same words repeatedly and not letting me sleep. I also cannot forget how his parents, sisters, and brothers gave me such a hard time which is still engraved in my heart as well as all the other cruel and selfish incidents that I was subjected to by almost everyone throughout my life.

For 35 years I had to put up with Sanjeev's daily verbal and physical abuse, the kind I only ever saw in movies and police shows. I used to think that all my bad memories should burn with me, including my rape, when I die. I was never able to tell anyone at that time, not even my sister, who I know would not have believed me. The second person that most people would be able to tell is their spouse, but I could not tell Sanjeev because he would have just insulted me even more. That is how he was, just like he had told everyone about my lack of education and degraded me by telling everyone that I could not read or write. He had even told a taxi driver that he wanted to divorce me because I was uneducated. This would just give him more reason to shame me in front of our family, neighbours, shopkeepers, the whole world, and anyone else he would talk to. That was the reason I was never able to tell him anything. I knew that he would ridicule me at any time instead of being sympathetic and understanding.

I started watching Dr. Phil's talk show, that I found therapeutic and healing. I listened to children and women talking about their abuses and their courage to speak out openly. I realized that I am not the only one who was in this situation and there are so many people in even worse situations than myself. The guests on the show say that after suffering in silence for so many years, they felt better sharing their story with others. So, in 2013, I started writing everything down so that I might feel better about my life. Instead of making myself feel better, I felt worse - like I had washed my dirty laundry in public. However, I slowly started sharing my life story with my children since I started writing, which has made me feel better. Having them all know the truth has released the guilt and pain hidden deep inside of me. I also feel a sense of relief that I no longer need to hide my painful journey which I was going to keep as a secret to my grave.

Now being older and wiser, I realize and learned, I was going through severe depression that was leading me to being suicidal. I think the creation of my pretend life was an outlet to escape from the entrapment of possibly going crazy. I am not depressed anymore.

One thing I still don't understand is why I was so wise and understanding in my pretend life but not in my real life. I taught my children wrong to right, to love each other and also defend each other from others. But in my real life I could not defend them from anyone, including Sanjeev. I could take the hurt he threw at me, but I could not open my mouth to defend them, and I hated myself for that.

I am also going to die hating God for making me this way, the same God that I used to pray to since I was very little. I still believe in God though. When Sanjeev was nice even for a week, I used to think that God had finally listened to my prayer. Now, when I see Asha suffering, unable to communicate and imprisoned in her own mind, it makes me question why God had made her unable to understand, what more he could want from her, and how much longer he wants to punish her. It does not matter how much I pray and have prayed for his help for Asha, he does not and has not listened to my prayers for her.

Watching Dr. Phil's program about young children getting tortured and raped for years and years, my heart goes out to them and I cannot stop crying when I watch. There is no escape for them and my pain seems to be a pinch compared to theirs. It makes me question why God can be so cruel and why he would not help them but just watches their pain and suffering. Where was God when they asked him to help them? I bet he was seeing how much more pain they could take.

Despite my anger and criticisms of God and even though at times I do not want to believe in him, I still pray. It is like a bad habit, like I hate my head, but I cannot separate it from my body. I fear God because if I had prayed so much to him and this is how my life resulted, what additional pain would I have been forced to endure if I had not prayed? Perhaps he was going to punish me even more. I do not want to lose or hurt any more than I already have.

At this point, I am just looking forward to leaving this world as if I would be going on an eternal dream vacation. I think I have lived too long now, and I am a burden even to myself. It was very cruel of me to even think that Asha should go before me, but at the same time it would also be cruel to burden my other children with her when I have lived my whole life that way. Her health is deteriorating as she gets older, and I feel that I do not have much longer to take care of her. But, I wish God does not make Asha suffer too long. I can only wish but in the end, whatever happens, will happen. I have started feeling content and looking forward to living the rest of my life in peace.

CHAPTER 22

It is now 2018 as I write this, and I am 76 years old. I had finished writing about my life in 2013 but God was not finished with me yet. He wanted to punish me to the end and where it would hurt me the most. That is why on August 9, 2014 he took my youngest daughter, Tara, away from me forever.

In 2012 Tara had started getting pneumonia twice a year, winter and summer, which was unusual in itself. The antibiotics her doctor prescribed had worked in the first year but not in the second year. Finally, at my advice, Tara pressured her doctor to send her to an oncologist. Instead, her doctor sent her for a TB test. Her doctor was fully aware that Tara had breast cancer 7 years ago and should be tested for lung cancer as persistent pneumonia was often the first sign in patients who previously had breast cancer. But she was negligent and uncaring because even when the TB test came back negative, she sent Tara for further TB tests. Obviously, it proved negative again.

Tara lived in Toronto and would call me almost every day and tell me she was feeling worse and had no energy as the days would go. I was getting very angry and frustrated at the doctor and suggested she find another one. Tara said it was too late to change doctors as all her medical history was with her current doctor. She did not want to go through all the testing all over again.

I felt like the doctor played with my daughter's life. She probably did not like Tara because she would not send her for the right diagnosis. Finally, when the doctor had no other choice, since the TB test results kept coming back negative, she sent her for lung cancer test. Three days later, the oncologist called her at 9:00p.m. at night and told her she had lung and bone cancer and she only had 3 months to live. When she phoned and told me, I could not believe what I heard. I was totally shocked. I asked how she felt. She was so calm and said she was okay, as if she already conceded to her fate.

She asked me to promise her that I would not force her to get any cancer treatments because she did not want to go through the chemo treatment again. She had resigned herself to die. No mother can ever be prepared to hear her child so sad, depressed, and wanting to die.

On the morning of August 1st, 2014, Tara phoned me again that something was wrong in her heart. Anjali and I went to see her that day. We were taken aback to see her looking so weak. She drank water with a spoon. I learned she had not told me everything; that she was in so much pain that she had to take morphine every two hours, and because she could not swallow, she had to crush them into powder before taking them. She had not eaten food for quite some time either. When I asked her why she kept this from me even if we talked on the phone every day, she said she did not want to worry me because I had enough worries and problems dealing with Asha.

We wanted to take her to the hospital, but she was not ready to go as she wanted to finish some work on her laptop. We stayed the night, worried about her. In the early hours of Sunday morning, around 3:00 a.m., she got even worse and was in so much pain that we had no choice but to rush her to the emergency room. They admitted her immediately. I stayed there the night and Anjali went back home. While Tara was in the hospital, Kajal had come just a few days earlier for a 3-week vacation from Texas. Kajal did not know the extent of Tara's condition since she had kept us all in the dark.

Tara's condition was deteriorating really fast, so we asked the palliative doctor why. He said her cancer was very aggressive and had spread very quickly so she did not actually have months to live but rather weeks. In truth, they hid the fact she only had a matter of days to live, which they did not reveal to us at that time.

I spent one or two nights with Tara, but not on the night she died. I was at home because we were celebrating my granddaughter, Priya's, birthday with Anjali. Kajal was staying with Tara that night and I was planning to stay the following night. However, Tara died in the early hours of Saturday, August 9th, 2014 at around 3:00a.m. Even though she died peacefully in her sleep, there was not enough time for us to make peace with her passing as she died within a week of being admitted to the hospital. I felt very upset that the doctors had not told us we only had a few days with her. If they had, I would have ensured that I stayed by her bed and spent every last moment with her. I still feel a lot of hurt and pain they did not tell us.

There is not a day that goes by that I do not remember Tara and how I failed my own daughter. How could she feel so sad and alone, to the point she wanted to die? And how I could not do anything to help her. I am also very angry at her doctor, whom I thought was heartless and uncaring. If she had tested Tara earlier, my daughter could have survived, or, at the very least, we could have had more precious time together. Why God does not punish those people who like to play with innocent people's lives, I will never understand.

As much as I am angry at her doctor, I am cursing myself more as it was my time to go and not my daughter's. Everyone was right, including Sanjeev, who said I was bad luck. All my life, I prayed to God for my children's safety and their happiness, yet God never seemed to hear. Since he took my daughter Tara and my teenage grand-daughter, Kiran, I feel hopeless and powerless even as I pray. I feel like I am not even free to ask God what I have done so badly and why He is punishing me because I am scared He would just punish me even more for asking Him. It seems as if the judge on earth and the god in heaven have the same rules. I think I am standing in court and the judge is giving me the sentence, but I cannot say anything because I fear that if I say I am not guilty he might give me an even longer sentence.

So, I cry in my heart, in closed rooms and behind my children's backs. No one can see me or hear me, like a thief in the dark so I wouldn't get caught and asked any questions about why I am crying and have to explain the sorrows of my heart.

CHAPTER 23

njali had started seeing someone in 2012 and as time went by, they wanted to live together along with his two children. Both her children, Priya and Rohan, have started universities in 2014 and 2015 as well. In October 2015 I had moved to an apartment with Asha as I did not want to interfere in her life. Anjali's boyfriend and his two children then moved in with her in November 2015. However, it did not last long, and they broke up in July 2016, but did try to reconcile a few times later.

During that time, my health had started weakening considerably and I could barely walk or stand because I was having so much pain. In December 2015 I had spine surgery, which helped relieve the pain in my legs. I could once again start walking and standing for longer periods of time.

As I went through many health problems, I continuously worried about Asha in case my health got worse. With the help of Arjun, Vibha and Anjali, I started looking for a place for her again and finally found a Long-Term Care Home (LTCH) in Oakville which accepted Asha in May 2016.

I settled Asha down in the LTCH, but I felt guilty that I abandoned her. The first few weeks were a bit hard for her to settle down, but eventually she did, which helped lessen the guilt I felt. I went to see Asha twice a day, every day, for the first month. I then hired a respite worker for the following month to go every morning for 2 hours to spend time with her and I would go every evening. After a couple of months, the nurse told me that I should not come every day, so Asha can settle down without me as she would eventually have to when I am gone. I now go to see Asha every other day and I think she has now also accepted she is going to stay there. The days I don't go, the respite worker goes there. I do continue to struggle and worry about her and the mere fact she will never understand why I would no longer see her when that time arrives, and I am gone. I also feel a sense of remorse, but I think this is the kindest way to leave her when I am gone.

I now live in the apartment alone. In these moments, I find myself always thinking about my life. I think about losing my daughter and my grand-daughter, when my whole life I had tried to be there for them. I had chosen not to kill myself to make sure they did not live a life without a mother or face the cruelties like I had. Some days are so bad that I cannot control my tears all day long. There are days when I try to distract myself by watching television, but the painful memories still come crushing down on me. My life was full of torment and stripped of a normal childhood and abandoned of any form of support or love. It also still haunts and pains me deeply about the man who raped me, even though it happened six decades ago; he damaged the very core of my soul, body and mind at such a young age that I cannot seem to heal the wound to this day and find myself still plagued by him even though I heard he already died.

So many sad and abusive incidents are still locked deep in the depths of my mind and it is hard for me to unlock and unleash them all for the fear of spiraling back into depression. It has been a long, difficult journey and has taken years for me to let go of the incidents mentioned in this book, but I can now say I no longer dwell too long or go back into that sad, lonely and harsh place of my life when those dark moments do resurface. I also rarely go back to my pretend life. And even when I do go there sometimes, there is no longer much interest as I had fulfilled everything in that life.

All I can say is the abuse I was subjected to day after day and month after month and year after year can never really heal completely. There will always be some form of scars left behind as reminders of how harsh, cruel and selfish some people can be. However, it is also a great reminder that I made it through those painful and dark times of my life and that I persevered so that I can now see that life can be beautiful and I can also look forward to seeing more happiness unfold through my children's and grandchildren's lives.

All my grandchildren are doing well. My eldest granddaughter, Neha, graduated with a medical degree in 2010 from Southampton University, England where she also met her husband Matt, who was studying medicine. They married in 2012 and she continued her studies to specialize in facial reconstruction surgery and graduated in 2018. Meanwhile, my other grandchildren, Rani, Sanjay and Rohit, from my eldest daughter, Kajal, had all gone to different universities in America and have all graduated and are holding very good jobs there. Anjali's children, Priya and Rohan are currently studying at different universities in Ontario, Canada and will be graduating in 2018 and 2019.

I feel very proud of all my children and grandchildren for what they have achieved, and it gives me great happiness that I persevered through all the dark times of my life. They have made me feel it was all worthwhile.

Printed in the United States
By Bookmasters